Life beyond

Suffering

"After the needs of survival have been met, what is left but the evolution of the soul?"-Kinzer

A 60 day extensive reading and journaling practice that includes a series of Meditations and Mental practices for transforming your mind and soul.

Preface

In this journal you will find many things, but most of all I wish to assist you in finding yourself. The aim of this book is simple, to help. Help build a routine, help you cast through your inner storm, help you create more space in your mind, and most of all help you live a better life. Through this journey that we will embark upon together we will reinvent what it means to have a journal. Everyday there will be practices for you as well as a small excerpt worth reading. The goal of these sixty days is not for me to show you the way, but rather through my words I wish to act as a guiding reflection for your own inner power and wisdom that you can tap into and channel. This book is designed purposefully to not take up too much of your time all the while being profoundly effective in its instructions and practices. This will be something you can depend upon as a checkpoint throughout your day. Together, we will discover the very depths of who you are and how we can gracefully love ourselves to fulfillment. The greatest teacher you will ever have is you. You hold all the power, and though I can attribute to this book my own growth as a person, it is ultimately you who will be the difference maker in your life. You are your own hero and you are your own healer. Now, I wait in excitement as you turn the page and begin your journey, I wish you the best of luck.

Are you ready to begin?

Day 1

Let's start with 5 things you are grateful for in your life

1. _____
2. _____
3. _____
4. _____
5. _____

Nice!

Now let's set an intention for today (Ex: To be kind or to be positive)

Intention for Day 1

_____

Great!

Now let's go over today's mental practice...

Throughout the next 60 days there will be a meditation practice for each day. So this will require you to find a quiet place for a small amount of time each day. If you miss a day, don't stress over it, but try to stay consistent! If you can't find a quiet place, use your headphones to put on some meditation music on Youtube. Though, silence is preferred. Todays practice will be 5 minutes long and you can find information for this practice on the following page.

"How do I meditate?"

We know that the mind is always going to run, some days faster than others. But as we know, some days they come at us at a speed we just can't handle. This may leave us feeling overwhelmed and anxious but this is normal. What we must do is learn to slow down the speed of these thoughts and how much they affect us when they do reach us. While in meditation, we practice gaining control of our awareness. It's like a game of remembering you're meditating when you're actually doing it. This is a process of getting stuck in thoughts and seeing how long it will take you to get unstuck and remember. Eventually our mind will become clearer, and less prone to thoughts as a whole which now puts us in a place to focus on thoughts we would actually like to think.

You are not your thoughts.

Through this process of sitting down, breathing, and becoming aware of our thoughts we must realize we in essence are not the thoughts. Our thinking is a product of many things such as environmental factors and biology. Thoughts are a product of the mind, not of the soul. You are the one who hears the thoughts, you are the one who is aware of them.

So as you sit down in a quiet room, close your eyes and follow your breath. In and out, slowly and comfortably. The mind will start to chatter and that's ok. Just try to come back to focusing on your breathing. Even if the whole five minutes you get lost in thinking and only manage to come back to focus once or twice it's ok. We now know that the act of stillness and attempted awareness itself is enough to affect the way our brains work when done daily!

I now invite you to practice said meditation as we finish our journaling for day number one. Set a timer for five minutes and practice following your breath.

Post Meditation Reflection: How did your meditation go?
(These will be fun to look at as you become a more skilled meditator.)

_____

_____

_____

_____

_____

_____

_____

Let us meet again for Day 2 :)

Day 2

Let's start with 5 things you are grateful for in your life

1. _____

2. _____

3. _____

4. _____

5. _____

Sweet!

Now let's set an intention for today...

Intention for Day 2

_____

Todays Mental Practice

Throughout the next 60 days there will be a meditation practice for each day. Like yesterday, today's meditation will be for a duration of five minutes. These practices will increase in length as the days go on. As well, consider your daily practice to affirm positive thoughts! More info on this on the following page.

Let's introduce you to **Positive Affirmations!**

"What are positive affirmations?"

Your subconscious mind operates differently than your conscious mind. The subconscious is like a computer following an algorithm. The more time and energy the conscious mind spends on a certain subject, the more important the subconscious mind believes this topic to be. That is why when we spend so much energy avoiding negative thoughts, we are actually showing our subconscious we would like to receive more of these thoughts. So the key isn't trying to control what thoughts we think, but to change our relationship with our thoughts as a whole. Your subconscious mind can actually be trained to be more positive all on its own. This comes from an increase of awareness. When we become more mindful of the thoughts we think, the words we say, and the actions we take, it creates room for change. After all, you can't change something if you are not aware of it. So through meditation we elevate our awareness, and the goal is to carry this awareness with us throughout our day. From this state of being, we can consciously choose to speak and act more positively. Remember, even if you are conscious of the practice at hand, that takes no effect on the training of the subconscious mind.

Let's break down the typical equation: A person will first usually **think** negative thoughts, which causes them to **speak** negatively, and then they will often **act** negatively to complete the equation.

As we can see it starts in the mind. This is the product of unconscious behavior. It's a cycle that will continue to run like code on a computer until something changes. That "something" is awareness. To make the change we desire, we are going to flip the equation on its head. We are going to consciously **speak** and **act** positive consistently showing our subconscious mind the kind of person we are. This will change the thoughts we receive naturally over time. This is the goal of positive affirmations. To affirm positivity often, in an attempt to train the brain and reverse the conditioning of negativity. In my experience, it takes a lot less time to untie the knots than to tie them. This is what makes this practice so beneficial and it is a practice we will consistently use in the coming days.

Now let's write down some positive affirmations (Ex: I am at peace or I consciously choose positivity, it is my natural state.) Remember to always refer to yourself in the present tense. This takes away the chasing of any sort of state of being and replaces it with an I AM statement. (A powerful choice of wording.)

Affirmations

1. _____
2. _____
3. _____
4. _____
5. _____

Post Meditation Reflection: How did your meditation go?

(These will be fun to look at as you become a more skilled meditator.)

_____

_____

_____

Let us meet again for Day 3 :)

Day 3

Let's start with 5 things you are grateful for in your life

1. _____
2. _____
3. _____
4. _____
5. _____

Awesome!

Now let's set an intention for today...

Intention for Day 3

_____

Todays Mental Practice

Throughout the next 60 days there will be a meditation practice for each day. Like yesterday, today's meditation will be for a duration of five minutes. These practices will increase in length as the days go on. Today, try to bring awareness to the space in between your thoughts, it is in that space where your inner intuition can guide you and where all the magic of synchronicities are forged.

"How do we create space?"

Creating space in our lives can look like a lot of different things. But it is only when we create space in our minds that we can grow as a person and evolve as beings of consciousness as well. Have you ever experienced a time in your life whether it was playing sports or practicing a craft or anything of that nature, but you found yourself almost lost in time? For a brief moment, it's as if your thinking brain was shut off and you were performing almost in a state of autopilot. This is what many refer to as the **flow state** and its magical process that we all have the capability of tapping into. It is in this flow, that we can become aligned with the natural direction of life. I invite you to think of the times you have entered flow state. It was probably the result of engaging in something you're very passionate about and that excites you. This can be accomplished as well when we are with a person or people that makes us feel really comfortable and happy. The flow is always there and it exists when we bring ourselves into harmony with things that excite us.

The flow is something nature knows all about, it's an intuitive intelligence that needs not further explaining. What we see is that when animals have their needs met (safety and food) their next concern is almost always play. This is the natural direction or flow of life, it is passion, excitement, and the unknown.

The path of least resistance will almost always lead you into the unknown, and until you make friends with change and the unknown, the depths of the flow are inaccessible. We can create space for the flow by withholding our judgment. Stop judging everything you think, hear, and see. Allow space between your awareness and the things you encounter in your daily life. When we become less judgemental and firm on how everything in our lives must be, we invite the magic that exists in the flow to surprise us and open new doors for us. (Ex: Synchronicities:)

Let's practice those affirmations again! This time I invite you to affirm your alignment with the flow of life. (Ex: I am one with the flow of life or Good things come to me and are attracted to me naturally.)

Affirmations

1. _____
2. _____
3. _____
4. _____
5. _____

Post Meditation Reflection: How did your meditation go?

(As well, consider writing a reflection upon creating space as we discussed earlier.)

_____

_____

_____

_____

_____

Let us meet again for Day 4 :)

Day 4

Let's start with 5 things you are grateful for in your life

1. _____
2. _____
3. _____
4. _____
5. _____

Great!

Now let's set an intention for today...

Intention for Day 4

_____

Todays Mental Practice

Throughout the next 60 days there will be a meditation practice for each day. Like yesterday, today's meditation will be for a duration of five minutes. These practices will increase in length as the days go on. The theme for today is gratitude, more info on this on the next page, but try welcoming your incoming meditation with a bit of thankfulness. Say aloud that you are grateful for the opportunity to find a space to elevate in such a way. Thank your higher self for placing you on the path you are on.

"Why is gratitude so important?"

Gratitude is one of the most powerful and magnetic states you can exist in. On a grounded level, becoming consciously grateful for the things around you allows you a deeper connection with life and those involved in it. As well, from an energy standpoint, gratitude is a state of receiving. When we can exist in gratitude, we invite the forces of the universe to further give us things to be grateful for. Think about it, would you want to give good gifts to someone who never appreciates the gesture? No! Of course not. You feel more inclined and happy to give someone gifts who deeply appreciates them and are thankful for them. Nonetheless, the universe acts as a mirror, so if you can consistently exist in a state of gratitude the universe rebounds more things for you to be grateful for simply because you are an energetic match to that frequency.

How can we apply this right now?

The most powerful and effective practice of any concept is not just pondering it but actually putting it into action. So let us change our relationship with life. Instead of us always asking and wanting to take from life, how can we be friends with it? When we tune into right now, and let the moment be exactly how it wishes to be and we tell ourselves we will love and be grateful for it either way, this creates a relationship with the universe that differs from previously. Now, there is harmony. As we talked about before, the universe acts as a mirror, and when you don't judge the reflections of this mirror, and instead love them for what they are, you invite beautiful things to happen to you.

Next, take action and put this process into initiation. Do not wait for something to cause you happiness to feel grateful. You be the cause for your happiness and be grateful for the opportunity to do such a thing. No more unconscious cause and effect. You are the cause and you choose the effect. Accept your role as a co creator of your reality, be grateful for the opportunity, and the universe will finally say in metaphor "nice, they finally get it."

Let's practice those affirmations again! This time incorporate gratitude. (Ex: I am grateful to be in alignment with my soul's purpose) This is powerful due to the fact that your affirmation empowers the soul while your gratitude grounds it, this creates a graceful balance.

Affirmations

1. _____
2. _____
3. _____
4. _____
5. _____

Post Meditation Reflection: How did your meditation go?

(As well, consider writing a reflection upon your relationship with gratitude as we discussed earlier.)

_____

_____

_____

_____

Let us meet again for Day 5 :)

Day 5

Let's start with 5 things you are grateful for in your life

1. _____
2. _____
3. _____
4. _____
5. _____

Sick!

Now let's set an intention for today...

Intention for Day 5

Todays Mental Practice

Throughout the next 60 days there will be a meditation practice for each day. Like yesterday, today's meditation will be for a duration of five minutes. These practices will increase in length as the days go on. Today's theme is forgiveness. So before you enter todays meditation, I'd like to think of where you're still holding anger and resentment. This is crucial for growth as a person and freedom of the soul, more info on the following page. Set the intention for your meditation to let go anywhere within you that is still making negative space for certain people. Ask your higher self to guide towards release in this regard.

"Why is forgiveness so important?"

We must learn to forgive, firstly, for selfish reasons. Which in reality isn't really selfish, more on the basis of self-love when approached correctly. At first it may be hard to forgive a certain person for what they did, but for long as we hold that space within us that contains the energy of resentment and anger, we will suffer, period. This is how energy within us becomes stuck. Energy isn't meant to be stagnant, it's meant to be flowing, so when we hold on to this energy in an attempt to nullify it, it's actually having the reverse effect. Forgiveness is not about denying ourselves of anger, it's about accepting that emotion and giving it the proper farewell. For long as we hold resentment, we are surrendering our power. Our focus and our energy is our greatest currency. So truly be honest with yourself about what it is you are angry about or who you hold resentment for. You can even come back to this reading in times of anger to help you calm down and remember not only who you are but who you want to be. Breathe deeply feeling the current emotion and welcome it into your home. How does it feel in your body? What does it make you want to do? The answer to these questions is found from the filtration of anger. So pay attention to your responses. Let the emotion in, for that is the only way it can exist. The only way for energy in motion (emotion) to pass is through you. Otherwise it will become stuck and cause problems. Some of which can even manifest physically if we hold on to them for long enough. Later on we will talk about why people act in certain ways, but for now let us set the intention for forgiveness for the sole reason of allowing stagnant energy to finally be released. Here is an affirmation you can practice since words as well carry energy. "I allow all emotion into my awareness, to be felt and to be let go of." Take this affirmation to heart and truly allow yourself to feel the hurt that another person has caused you. Here's the secret ingredient to make it all come together. Are you ready? Love the part of you that is hurt. Love the part of you that feels anger. Love the part of you that wants revenge. Do not fall victim to thinking this emotion is who you are. You reside in a place of higher consciousness, and with love you can illuminate the darkness within you. By softening yourself, and allowing, you will see that energy can be transmuted and let go of.

Let's practice those affirmations again! This time include forgiveness in your intended affirmations. (Ex: I forgive those who have wronged me, I allow myself to feel and release negative emotion.)

Affirmations

1. _____
2. _____
3. _____
4. _____
5. _____

Post Meditation Reflection: How did your meditation go?

(As well, consider writing a reflection upon forgiveness as we discussed earlier.)

_____

_____

Let us meet again for Day 6 :)

Day 6

Let's start with 5 things you are grateful for in your life

1. _____
2. _____
3. _____
4. _____
5. _____

Sweet!

Now let's set an intention for today...

Intention for Day 6

_____

Todays Mental Practice

Throughout the next 60 days there will be a meditation practice for each day. Like yesterday, today's meditation will be for a duration of five minutes. These practices will increase in length as the days go on. Today's theme is internal kindness. Before entering your meditation set the intention to be kind to yourself and allow yourself the patience to sit through whether thoughts and emotions you may be having. Remember you are the awareness of these things.

"What is internal kindness?"

Our innerspace is our home, and as we navigate our way through thoughts, emotions, and belief systems that have been formed over the many years of unconscious living, it is our responsibility to be kind to ourselves throughout the whole process. Truthfully, if you wage war on yourself you hit many roadblocks. Because though many times in life we are required to be brave and persevere through adversity, this won't work at the higher levels of awareness and consciousness. You can not hate your way into changing, you can only love yourself into evolution. This is often why people who struggle with anxiety and overthinking have such a hard time. These types of people are often those who like to have control, and there is no inherent problem with that but when it comes to innerspace as well as our relationship with external reality we must learn to surrender. We must learn to move with grace rather than force. So I would like you for a minute to consider the voice that resides in your head. You probably know it all too well, you may even believe it to be you. But as we mentioned before, this voice isn't you. It is a product of the mind. You are beyond just this voice, but it is still a part of you. So now it's time to establish a relationship with this voice. The voice may offer some good ideas and insights sometimes, or it may be extremely intolerable with its negativity. I'd like you to create some space between you and the voice and now see this as a partnership rather than a singular narrative. When the voice in your head starts chatting once again, observe it as you would in meditation, and treat it as someone you love very dearly. Love this voice unconditionally. Even when it sputes nonsense that triggers you, thank it for bringing these triggers to your attention, for that is the only way you can transcend them. Every thought that triggers you is a call for help from your subconscious and when you react with love and kindness instead of fear, the entire dynamic of your inner space changes. After a good amount of time, that voice will start to embody the love and kindness you have shown it. All our minds ever wish to do is serve us. Your mind is far from your enemy, it is your greatest companion and tool if you allow it to be. Treat that voice the way you wish for it to speak to you, with love and kindness.

Let's practice those affirmations again! This time include kindness in your intended affirmations. (Ex: I treat myself with love and kindness always) This may feel "corny" to some of you, but this is just a practice for you to hear that inner voice be positive. For those who only know a negative inner voice, this is an instrumental practice if you allow it to be.

Affirmations

1. _____
2. _____
3. _____
4. _____
5. _____

Post Meditation Reflection: How did your meditation go?

(As well, consider writing a reflection upon internal kindness as we discussed earlier.)

_____

_____

Let us meet again for Day 7 :)

Day 7

Let's start with 5 things you are grateful for in your life

1. _____

2. _____

3. _____

4. _____

5. _____

Nice!

Now let's set an intention for today...

Intention for Day 7

Todays Mental Practice

Throughout the next 60 days there will be a meditation practice for each day. Like yesterday, today's meditation will be for a duration of five minutes. These practices will increase in length as the days go on. Today's theme is external kindness. I invite you to do a kind gesture for someone today. Even if it is something as small as opening the door for them or giving a friend a compliment.

"What is external kindness?"

Yesterday we talked about being kind to ourselves and I purposefully put that before external kindness because the two go hand in hand. Though, I believe we can not truly feel the connection of external kindness and its impacts until we have learned internal kindness as well. In truth, once internal kindness is practiced and prioritized, external kindness is effortless. We are always projecting our inner reality to create our external reality, so in this sense when one is kind to themselves they can be kind to others without even saying a word. That is because our presence holds an energy, and when our inner space is one of kindness and love, this energy is projected outwards into the hearts of those we surround ourselves with. Now to others, unconsciously, we are extending them an invitation to love and be kind to themselves. This may sound a bit confusing, but this is yet again a game of energy. We don't really need to understand how it works to know it works. The reason your energy is an invitation for others to go back within themselves instead of just immersing themselves in your energy is because they aren't you. Though you have practiced being kind to yourself, this may look different than how another person must practice being kind to themselves. We all have different levels of baggage that we carry through life and we all have different relationships with our inner voice. This is why everything starts within, and absolutely everything is a projection of our relationship with ourselves. So if you truly want to make a difference in the lives of those around you, be kind and love yourself to a great degree. Exist in this state of being and simply go about things as you normally would, don't overthink it. You will find yourself naturally serving others in a kind manner unconsciously, just like your unconscious mind serves you kindly when this type of relationship is established and the healing process takes initiative. It is all a reflection, it is all a mirror of our own state of being and our own self love.

Let's practice those affirmations again! This time include kindness in your intended affirmations. (Ex: I naturally invite others to be kind and loving through my own kindness and self love.)

Affirmations

1. _____
2. _____
3. _____
4. _____
5. _____

Post Meditation Reflection: How did your meditation go?

(As well, consider writing a reflection upon external kindness as we discussed earlier.)

_____

_____

_____

_____

_____

Let us meet again for Day 8 :)

Day 8

Let's start with 5 things you are grateful for in your life

1. _____
2. _____
3. _____
4. _____
5. _____

Great!

Now let's set an intention for today...

Intention for Day 8

Todays Mental Practice

Throughout the next 60 days there will be a meditation practice for each day. Like yesterday, today's meditation will be for a duration of five minutes. These practices will increase in length as the days go on. Today's theme is patience. I invite you to go the extra mile today in terms of your patience. Really stay conscious of things that cause emotional imbalance, and ask yourself "is this really worth my reaction?

"Why is patience so important?"

You've now spent a week meditating for five minutes a day. I'm not going to assume you see improvements, but maybe the very act of getting yourself to sit down and do nothing has become easier. Patience is so very important in regards to our relationship with ourselves as well as our relationship with life. Let us look at nature, nothing is ever in a rush, yet everything gets done nonetheless. I will tell you this now and this may be a hard pill to swallow. There is not really any sort of finish line. You may think you've overcome a certain thought pattern or behavior but it may return and that's ok. There is no miracle cure, and if there is a miracle cure, the closest thing to it is the acceptance that there isn't a miracle cure. This is why it is so important to have something like meditation to come back to in times of chaos. Meditation allows us to be patience itself, it allows us to momentarily be nothing. Patience is really the act of carrying this little bit of nothingness with us throughout our day. Though something may upset you, understand that it upset **YOU** the person, not you the awareness/soul. The you that is beyond the thinking mind, the you that is merely an aspect of the flow, can not run out of patience, it is impossible. You may be thinking this is all a bit crazy for understanding the effectiveness of patience, but really what I'm trying to show you is that when we remain conscious of the grand scheme of things, many smaller ordeals become not worth getting angry over. You have a small amount of time on this planet and instead of saying "he called me this" or "she did that to me" back up for a minute, come back to the greater truth, and debate whether this is worth entering an emotional state you don't enjoy being in. Usually it's not. Remember that you are the being beyond thoughts and emotions, and to fall into negative thought and emotions is always a choice, always. There will be times in life where getting upset is viable. It's natural to feel, as we've talked about earlier, but how we move forward dictates the ripples we create in outer reality. Remember, every action in a certain emotion, reinforces the universe mirroring further events carrying this emotion towards you. Why do you think you see the same people always upset in your life? I'm sure you know a couple people that get upset very quickly and basically surrender being happy because of a small inconvenience. The universe as it is a mirror, simply reflects our reactions back to us in the form of events and others. You are at that frequency, alignment is but certain. The key is remaining conscious, ninety-nine percent of the time things simply aren't worth surrendering your peace. This realization is what forges patience.

Let's practice those affirmations again! This time incorporate patience as a theme. (Ex: I will be patient with others today, I am a patient conscious being.)

Affirmations

1. _____
2. _____
3. _____
4. _____
5. _____

Post Meditation Reflection: How did your meditation go?

(As well, consider writing a reflection upon patience as we discussed earlier.)

_____

_____

Let us meet again for Day 9 :)

Day 9

Let's start with 5 things you are grateful for in your life

1. _____
2. _____
3. _____
4. _____
5. _____

Awesome!

Now let's set an intention for today...

Intention for Day 9

Todays Mental Practice

Throughout the next 60 days there will be a meditation practice for each day. Like yesterday, today's meditation will be for a duration of five minutes. These practices will increase in length as the days go on. Today's theme is learning how to live from the heart. This theme is an important one with many levels, I look forward to reflecting upon these levels with you.

"How do we live from the heart?"

Sooner or later, or whether you already know, you will see that love is the foundation for life. Any great master or teacher worth listening to will tell you the same thing. This is because when you strip the layers of the self, you are left with very little. But that which is seen as very little is actually absolutely everything. Everything is love. Love is the absolute positive polarity to existence. Love is unity, whilst lack of it is separation. Separation is an illusion. This is why when people start to "wake up" to their true nature as not only a human but something much more, they think to themselves "how could I have been so naive?" How could I have possibly been so forgetful?" Your essence, your soul, is pure vibrant love. This becomes clear when you actually start walking the path. When you start having experiences you can't explain. When you feel the oneness during one of your meditations. Love is a frequency, and it is where our higher self is attuned. If you ever are in question of how far you have strayed from your highest path, simply ask yourself how far you have strayed from love? Self love, love for others, and love for the experience of life. I'm not going to sit here and tell you that overnight your entire life will change simply from reading this, but I will say that if you remain conscious and hold and choose love consistently, your life will change. This is actually how we start living from the heart, by letting ourselves be a bit vulnerable. Allowing ourselves to get excited about things and to act on those things out of pure passion. In the following two days we will talk about self love as well as projected love. Every excerpt of this journal can be taken in relation to love. When asked about the universe's intentions for the places it takes you, see this notion; it is always about love or the lack of love. You from a place of higher consciousness, you in the frequency of pure love, calls these moments forward in the form of reality. The closer you are to this frequency, the more in alignment you will always be.

Let's practice those affirmations again! This time incorporate love, or maybe take role as you are in alignment with your highest self. (Ex: I am always in highest alignment with my soul)

Affirmations

1. _____
2. _____
3. _____
4. _____
5. _____

Post Meditation Reflection: How did your meditation go?

(As well, consider writing a reflection upon living from the heart as we discussed earlier.)

_____

_____

_____

_____

_____

Let us meet again for Day 10 :)

Day 10

Entering the double digits woo hoo!

Let's start with 5 things you are grateful for in your life

1. _____
2. _____
3. _____
4. _____
5. _____

Sweet!

Now let's set an intention for today...

Intention for Day 10

Todays Mental Practice

Throughout the next 60 days there will be a meditation practice for each day. Like yesterday, today's meditation will be for a duration of five minutes. These practices will increase in length as the days go on. Today's theme is self love. If you think self love is corny, then I ask you to see past your conditioning. Self love is everything. Someone who truly loves themselves is of great service to humanity. Genuine love not narcissistic love, more info on this on the following page.

"What is "self" love?"

Get any idea of what self love is out of your head. Because the self love we must practice transcends just the "self" as we know it. To truly love yourself, you must love yourself beyond just the person you play in reality. You must love your inner presence. You must venture into the universe that is your consciousness to realize the universe that exists within you is the same universe that exists outside of you. Inside of you, exists all the love that can ever be felt. An unconditional thread of energy that exists at your core. So to love yourself isn't just a healthy practice that can help with your mental health, it's the truth. When you love yourself, truly, you have cracked the code. Love more than just the face you see, love the very presence of your beingness. Love who is inside of the body. Even your thoughts and emotions from which you may have once identified with, you can love them as well. Once you see that you are so much greater and more connected than just a human on a rock in the middle of space, everything comes together.

How do we practice self love?

We can practice self love in many ways, but there is no greater way than remaining conscious. Remaining aware of who we are at our core and extending this knowledge to consciously move forward in love throughout our day. Love is a frequency, it's our natural bare state when stripped of all outer layers. All that is needed is an intention to reside and act from this frequency, all else to fall into place. Self love is also about respect. Respecting yourself enough to know where you're not valued and respecting yourself enough to have boundaries. Rather remove your presence from a person or place than remove your love. As well, love in its authenticity doesn't always look like a smile and a helping hand. Some days you're tired, you've had a long day, you are allowed to want to rest and recharge. Remember this is a game of energy. You need to be mindful of yours. Learn to be confident in your energy, though this is effortless when residing in or close to the frequency of love. Self love is really just love. In reality there is no other kind of love. Even when you love another, you are just experiencing your true nature as love mirrored in this person. This goes both ways. The more love one has for themselves, the more love they extend to another. Or in other words, the more love one has for themselves the more they can energetically invite another to tap into their true nature as love as well. I hope you understand the importance of this topic, it's the building blocks to everything. You must carry this lesson with you in all other lessons, or you will be circled back, because it's always about love or a lack thereof. Oneness is love, creation is love, art is love. These are different forms of the same frequency. Love is the final destination. The only thing another person can ever do for you is mirror the love you have inside of you. Once this concept is understood and practiced, everything changes. We will circle back to this theme more within the following days, cementing its importance and establishing an understanding of it through experience.

Let's practice those affirmations again! This time simply say "I am love," or "I exist in the frequency of love." Allow this mantra to be in your guiding point of balance.

Affirmations

1. _____
2. _____
3. _____
4. _____
5. _____

Post Meditation Reflection: How did your meditation go?

(As well, consider writing a reflection upon self love as we discussed earlier.)

Let us meet again for Day 11 :)

Day 11

Let's start with 5 things you are grateful for in your life

1. _____
2. _____
3. _____
4. _____
5. _____

Great!

Now let's set an intention for today...

Intention for Day 11

_____

Todays Mental Practice

Throughout the next 60 days there will be a meditation practice for each day. You have reached the **second level** of our meditation practice! I invite you to bump your meditation now to ten minutes. This may feel like a big jump, but remember to observe your discomfort and if it's not easy you're probably doing something right! Today's theme is projected love. Before your meditation ask your higher self to navigate you in ways in which you can feel and experience your true nature as love.

"What is projected love?"

We've discussed that all love stems from inside of us, but now how does this relate to being a loving person? A valid question that may arise is, "Kinzer, I understand we are all connected, but I don't feel love for everyone. Am I doing something wrong?" The answer is no. In truth, if your attention is towards loving others and learning how to do so, you're never in the wrong place. Loving others unconditionally sounds impossible, and it is difficult there is no denying that. I can't tell you that I have accomplished this feat, actually far from it. But just because the degree of difficulty is high, doesn't make the concept false. I don't believe our mission here on this planet is to master unconditional love, but rather to accept and understand love. As humans, loving others with conditions is all we know. But love transcends just humanity. Everything on earth and beyond is formulated in the frequency of love. Now, this frequency may be altered to show something else, or even the opposite polarity as we judge it to be. Again, this is a game of energy and frequencies, loving someone you don't know doesn't make sense to you as a singular person. But to your higher self, it's only natural. Your higher self does not see or feel oneness, it is oneness. There is no other, there is only one. The frequency of love is the final layer of the onion, though all other layers of the onion are still embedded in the same frequency. Just like how every person seems to be operating separately it's really the same energy divided into many parts. Everyone has an energy they are emitting, all attuned to different frequencies in relation to the one bare frequency of love. Think about humans as radios, all attuned to hyper specific radio channels. But now imagine that every broadcast is just playing different variations of the same song. This song is the frequency of love. We are all expressions of the same energy, slightly unique and different, and this is what makes each of us so special. So now when you look into the eyes of another person, see love, see light. Anybody that is here, is supposed to be here. Everyone is perfect already, because they are the frequency of love in motion. People may want to improve themselves and do whatever it is they want but that will never change the fact that they are perfect just the way they are. Everything is. We are like one big frequency family:) Except there is only one of us, and we are all it. I know I just threw a lot at you and not all of it has to make sense right about now. But just know that the natural direction and flow of life is love. Once you get a taste, playing it cool just seems trivial. But this is how love is projected, or rather connected. Tune into the frequency of love, and act from there. Don't do things for love, do them from love. Yes, it's going to be difficult. Love is the curriculum for your evolution as a soul. Here's a tip, it's not supposed to feel like work. It's supposed to be fun, exciting, and light. If it is not that, take a step back and come into balance. Conscious authentic intention of acting in the frequency of love, is more beneficial than pretending to love everyone. Forge it within you, and allow it to project itself naturally. That's what it does, its positive energy, it projects. You can imprint your energetic signature on everywhere you go, often without having to even say a word.

Let's practice those affirmations again! This time, write whatever feels right.

Affirmations

1. _____
2. _____
3. _____
4. _____
5. _____

Post Meditation Reflection: How did your meditation go?

(As well, consider writing a reflection upon projected love as we discussed earlier.)

_____

_____

_____

_____

_____

_____

_____

Let us meet again for Day 12 :)

Day 12

Let's start with 5 things you are grateful for in your life

1. _____

2. _____

3. _____

4. _____

5. _____

Nice!

Now let's set an intention for today...

Intention for Day 12

_____

Todays Mental Practice

Throughout the next 60 days there will be a meditation practice for each day. You are now on the second level of our meditation practice and today's meditation will be ten minutes like yesterday. These meditations will get longer as the days go on. Today's theme is being grounded, so if you can take the time to be in nature and remind yourself that you are one with nature as well.

"Why is being grounded so important?"

Thus far, we've talked a lot about energy, frequencies, and things of that nature, but it's important not to get too lost in this world. We are always looking to elevate our consciousness but we should do so whilst also strengthening our roots. Just like a tree must cement its roots deep underground in the darkness so it can grow towards the heavens. We are the same, and I think a lot of the time you will see people be a bit too invested in the world we can't see with our eyes that they forget the whole point of the world we can see. Your experience here in reality, the one you can touch, feel, see, taste, and hear is always of utmost importance. After all you are here for a reason, you chose to come here, your higher self that is. So do not lose touch with reality and the things involved in it. The point of having deep spiritual insights is to help us transform our experience here on earth, not transcend it. You will see that the path will often invite you back into places you remove yourself from in the hopes that now you can appreciate it more greatly for what it is in truth and what you are in truth. We venture into a place of elevated consciousness to bring this knowledge down with us into our lives. In a way, if we were only ever operating from a very high frequency we might actually have some trouble in this life experience. That is why balance is necessary, and even when things are really good or really bad we can keep a sort of balance within that doesn't make the scale tip over. Being grounded also means being present, and this is something we practice during meditation. Living in reality, rather than believing the narrative our mind is telling us. Being in the present moment is of utmost importance, and it is something we will dive into a bit later, but there is never anywhere else to be but the present moment. If you can ground yourself in this moment, and truly be present in a flow state yet conscious type of awareness, you will truly be tapped into your highest alignment, your highest path.

Let's practice those affirmations again! This time, write whatever feels right.

Affirmations

1. _____
2. _____
3. _____
4. _____
5. _____

Post Meditation Reflection: How did your meditation go?

(As well, consider writing a reflection upon being grounded as we discussed earlier.)

_____

_____

_____

_____

_____

_____

Let us meet again for Day 13 :)

Day 13

Let's start with 5 things you are grateful for in your life

1. _____

2. _____

3. _____

4. _____

5. _____

Sweet!

Now let's set an intention for today...

Intention for Day 13

_____

Todays Mental Practice

Throughout the next 60 days there will be a meditation practice for each day. You are now on the second level of our meditation practice and today's meditation will be ten minutes like yesterday. These meditations will get longer as the days go on. Today's theme is understanding how holding on hurts more than letting go.

"Holding on hurts more than letting go?"

Holding on to negative emotions whether it be from the past or the present can be detrimental, let me offer an example. Imagine you are hanging from a pull up bar that is very high up, you can't see where you would land so you're scared to let go. Eventually you will start to lose grip and your hands will start hurting. After some time passes your whole body starts to ache from holding on for so long, you don't know how much longer you can go on like this. Your friend who says he has been in the same position as you tells you to let go. He tells you the fall isn't that bad and looks way scarier from the top. You trust him and see no reason as to why he would lie to you. You start to feel yourself losing grip, and eventually you have no choice but to let go. You scream from the fear of falling, and you see nothing but darkness on the way down. When suddenly your friend who you trust says "it's all going to be ok." At that moment, you feel relieved. Not because you know what you're about to hit at the bottom, but because you have no control over what happens, so you finally feel your body relax. Then in a split second you hit the bottom and it's a perfectly soft net to break your fall. You feel no pain, and realize the whole time you felt more hurt when you were holding on to the pull up bar for dear life.

What's the analogy referring to?

You may have been able to guess how this analogy plays a role in how we hold on to baggage from the past instead of letting go. Like a free fall, letting go means allowing ourselves to venture into the unknown. The thought of leaving a familiar suffering for an unknown result can be daunting on our subconscious but we need to override this using our intention. We need to allow ourselves to feel all the darkness, just as we would once falling from the pull up bar. This analogy can actually help in a multitude of ways including when dealing with overthinking or anxiety. Instead of trying to hold on for dear life, stop fighting, and just surrender. Let the unknown take you, ride the wave, don't try to control it. You'll see that the fear of letting yourself feel that certain emotion was scarier than actually feeling the emotion itself. The unknown is our friend when we don't try to control it.

Let's practice those affirmations again! This time, write whatever feels right.

Affirmations

1. _____
2. _____
3. _____
4. _____
5. _____

Post Meditation Reflection: How did your meditation go?

(As well, consider writing a reflection upon holding on vs letting go as we discussed earlier.)

_____

_____

_____

_____

Let us meet again for Day 14 :)

Day 14

Let's start with 5 things you are grateful for in your life

1. _____
2. _____
3. _____
4. _____
5. _____

Awesome!

Now let's set an intention for today...

Intention for Day 14

_____

Todays Mental Practice

Throughout the next 60 days there will be a meditation practice for each day. You are now on the second level of our meditation practice and today's meditation will be ten minutes like yesterday. These meditations will get longer as the days go on. Today's theme is bravery. I'd like you to think of either a time in your life you had to be brave or someone in your life you know you have to be brave for. Feel the empowering energy of this intention, and carry it with you in perseverance for the coming days.

"Why is it important to be brave?"

The universe grants favor to those who are bold. The universe is experiencing itself through us, so where do you think it is more likely to focus its energy? To those who are willing to experience the unknown beyond normal comfort. The entire foundation of this unfolding of life is to learn, to experience that which has not yet been experienced. And though now it seems as if everything has already been experienced, that couldn't be further from the truth. Even if I experience a certain event, the way I experience it will be different than the way you experience it. But this frequency of divine excitement and curiosity can only be reached when we venture into the depths of the unknown. It can only be felt when we are brave enough to open ourselves to it. Only when we become empowered and use our love for the experience of life to persevere through roadblocks do we feel this powerful energy. Again, the frequency of love, slightly tuned to a different degree. After all, the universe, consciousness, wishes to experience itself out of love for itself. Life is simply the experience of the many different octaves of love. And when you are willing to feel this love, when you are willing to own it, the flame within you begins to grow. So don't be afraid to leave your comfort zone, actually, take initiative to do just that. Because what happens is we actually grow a tolerance to discomfort. If someone who deals with anxiety never left their home, the one time they did leave their home they would most likely feel extremely anxious the whole time. So in this sense it takes bravery to leave the house everyday. Just because anxiety and fear is there, doesn't mean you have to listen to it. When we consistently leave our comfort zone often, that fire within us starts to grow. Our conscious mind is taking rulership over our subconscious. We are not letting anxiety and fear lead our life, rather we are being led by a wanting to come closer to a feeling within us. A freedom that can only be unlocked when we feed it. So yes, there will be moments when you are afraid. There will be moments that trigger your anxiety and maybe even your trauma, but how will you decide to move forward? Will you be brave?

Let's practice those affirmations again! This time, write whatever feels right.

Affirmations

1. _____
2. _____
3. _____
4. _____
5. _____

Post Meditation Reflection: How did your meditation go?

(As well, consider writing a reflection upon bravery as we discussed earlier.)

_____

_____

_____

_____

Let us meet again for Day 15 :)

Day 15

Let's start with 5 things you are grateful for in your life

1. _____
2. _____
3. _____
4. _____
5. _____

Great!

Now let's set an intention for today...

Intention for Day 15

_____

Todays Mental Practice

Throughout the next 60 days there will be a meditation practice for each day. You are now on the second level of our meditation practice and today's meditation will be ten minutes like yesterday. These meditations will get longer as the days go on. Today's theme is triggers. Think of things that may trigger you. Whether from a place of overthinking or just past experiences. Today we will go over what triggers are and tomorrow how to overcome them.

"What are triggers?"

Whatever it is you struggle with internally, you have certainly encountered triggers. Triggers are situations, conversations, or even synchronicities that trigger exactly what it is you struggle with. They actually exist to set you free. As much as they make you uncomfortable, it is the universe providing you the opportunity to heal and let go of whatever blockages you are still holding on to. Of course the universe would do this, because you are the universe, and you would provide yourself with that opportunity wouldn't you? Whenever something triggers you whether you've experienced this particular trigger for a while or it is a new one, it is simply the universe showing you that there is somewhere within you that needs healing and releasing. When a trigger is seen or felt, it is important to become aware. I often like to close my eyes and open myself up to whatever the incoming feeling may bring. I then breathe slowly and feel whatever it is I must without engaging in the tantalizing conversation the trigger would like to engage in. It's important you don't run or avoid these triggers because this will show your brain and the universe that you are not yet ready to evolve past these particular issues. You need to be brave, you need to sit in the storm, and just feel all the emotion it brings. The truth is, these blockages that exist within you are not going anywhere until they've been felt. Now, why are they called blockages? Every internal struggle you believe you deal with is simply energies you are holding onto. When you choose not to feel, energy says "well i'll just camp out here until they're ready to let me leave." Energy doesn't like being held captive and restricted. So the "demons" that you deal with, don't even want to be your demons! It's energy that wants to flow freely, but you're not letting it because you are too afraid to feel the emotion they will carry with them on their way out. Triggers are opportunities. Once you adopt this mindset, growth can once again continue. A big thing to draw your awareness to is how triggers affect your decision making. This energy has been haunting you for so long, you may now even make decisions to avoid running into said triggers. This is now a whole other level of fearful living. All created by you. You've created the narrative that somehow if you feel the emotion that the trigger carries something bad will happen. It's simply not true.

Let's practice those affirmations again! This time, write whatever feels right.

Affirmations

1. _____
2. _____
3. _____
4. _____
5. _____

Post Meditation Reflection: How did your meditation go?
(As well, consider writing a reflection upon triggers as we discussed earlier.)

_____

_____

_____

_____

_____

_____

_____

_____

Let us meet again for Day 16 :)

Day 16

Let's start with 5 things you are grateful for in your life

1. _____
2. _____
3. _____
4. _____
5. _____

Sweet!

Now let's set an intention for today...

Intention for Day 16

_____

Todays Mental Practice

Throughout the next 60 days there will be a meditation practice for each day. You are now on the second level of our meditation practice and today's meditation will be ten minutes like yesterday. These meditations will get longer as the days go on. Today's theme is overcoming triggers, this is a continuation of yesterday's theme!

"How do we overcome triggers?"

See past the fearful mind and be brave enough to trust the healing process. Often energy blockages are associated with tightness and that's a pretty accurate representation. When people are often anxious or worrisome they tighten their bodies up and there's no sense of relaxation and flow. Well, I'm here to tell you, life likes to flow. Like a stream of water, life likes to ever so continue its creative journey through all its vessels. By life, of course I mean the unfolding expression of consciousness experiencing its own creation. When you step in the way of this process by resisting change, not feeling your emotions truly, or even staying in a place you don't feel valued, this is where blockages are created. You must always remember to build your resilience and never your resistance. When a trigger makes itself apparent, open yourself to it. Let the feeling pass through you and not past you, and when that uncomfortable feeling does arise, observe that part of yourself and send it love. You may even want to say the affirmation "I see you, I accept you as part of me, and I love you." Your brain sees this and says "my human isn't scared of this, I guess there is nothing to worry about." The universe sees this, and says to you what you have said to yourself. The universe says "finally, that part of myself is ready to heal (you), I accept that part of myself and love that part of myself unconditionally." Do you see the oneness and flow of this whole process? You are an extension of the universe. You are not a person learning to let go, you are the universe remembering its true state of being. You're not learning anything new, you're simply remembering. Now, the next time you see a trigger, see it as a grand opportunity to let go and finally heal the blockages you've been wanting to let go of.

Let's practice those affirmations again! This time, write whatever feels right.

Affirmations

1. _____
2. _____
3. _____
4. _____
5. _____

Post Meditation Reflection: How did your meditation go?

(As well, consider writing a reflection upon overcoming triggers as we discussed earlier.)

_____

_____

_____

_____

_____

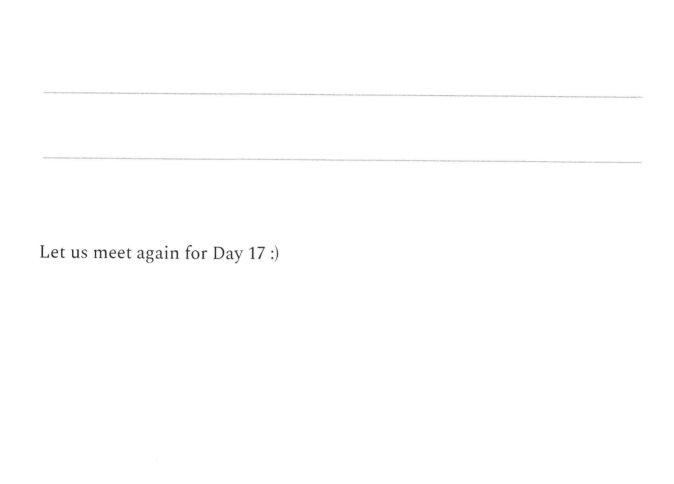

Let us meet again for Day 17 :)

Day 17

Let's start with 5 things you are grateful for in your life

1. _____

2. _____

3. _____

4. _____

5. _____

Awesome!

   Now let's set an intention for today...

Intention for Day 17

_____

Todays Mental Practice

   Throughout the next 60 days there will be a meditation practice for each day. You are now on the second level of our meditation practice and today's meditation will be ten minutes like yesterday. These meditations will get longer as the days go on. Today's theme is examining what exactly thoughts are...

"What are thoughts?"

Yikes, big question right? What exactly are thoughts? Well, thoughts are a product of our mind firstly. We know that our true nature is beyond mind, we are the awareness of mind. Our brain acts like a magnet ever so pulling in thoughts based on our state of being. So a person who is residing in the vibratory emotion of fear, will receive more fearful thoughts. It's kind of like an algorithm in a way. So where exactly is your mind pulling these thoughts from? Your mind, acting like a magnet for your state of being, is pulling in thoughts from consciousness. See that there is your individual consciousness, or rather just focused consciousness that is being made aware of, and there is flowing outer consciousness from which infinite thoughts, ideas, and daydreams exist. Thoughts are merely vessels for emotions to be made aware of. Emotions is the spectrum from which we exist, this spectrum is what is used to align you with the "random" thoughts that you receive from the flowing outer consciousness. So if we want to get rid of bad thoughts, we need to change the way we feel. How we feel is what is creating vibratory matches to the experiences in our life, not the thoughts we think. A good example is a person who is deaf, unable to hear, would still be pulling in and attracting experiences based on their state of being. A person who has never heard language would not think in words. Therefore thoughts are merely a costume emotions wear to make their existence known to us. Emotion (energy in motion) likes to keep in motion. So emotion that is being resisted within us, will use thoughts to create disturbance in our awareness, this disturbance can lead to us either feeling and letting go of the emotion or blaming our brain for having "bad" thoughts. I think you can see the clear choice to be made. So thoughts were never the problem, rather the emotion they carry that we are resistant to feeling. When you start to act as a third party to the thoughts you hear in your mind, and not be so dragged in and conquered by the emotion they bring, you can separate yourself from them. You can reside in awareness. From here, you can allow the thoughts to say whatever they want, keeping yourself open to the feelings they ignite and understanding by patiently waiting you can allow the thoughts to tire themselves out and all you will be left with is the emotion you've been avoiding. Staying open to feel and hurt if you must in order to set this emotion (energy) free is the way to go about this process. Thoughts are like notifications our subconscious sends to us to alert us of the emotions we are feeling. By keeping ourselves open and not judging the thoughts, we allow all feelings to move through us. For the only way emotion can be released is by us letting it through. You are not your thoughts, you are the awareness of them.

Let's practice those affirmations again! This time, write whatever feels right.

Affirmations

1. _____
2. _____
3. _____
4. _____
5. _____

Post Meditation Reflection: How did your meditation go?

(As well, consider writing a reflection upon what thoughts really are as we discussed earlier.)

Let us meet again for Day 18 :)

Day 18

Let's start with 5 things you are grateful for in your life

1. _____
2. _____
3. _____
4. _____
5. _____

Nice!

    Now let's set an intention for today...

Intention for Day 18

Todays Mental Practice

Throughout the next 60 days there will be a meditation practice for each day. You are now on the second level of our meditation practice and today's meditation will be ten minutes like yesterday. These meditations will get longer as the days go on. Today's theme is judgment. I invite you to think of some things or people in your life that you may have judged incorrectly in the past.

"How do we approach Judgment?"

Judgment is once again a reflection of the relationship we have with ourselves. In fact, pretty much everything in reality is a reflection of the relationship we have with ourselves. We often judge the very things we suppress in ourselves. Otherwise, if we had no connection to the very thing we were judging we simply wouldn't judge it. If you see a person walking down the street with a rather interesting outfit, what would be your reaction? Many people would turn to judgment, they'd say "look at that guy's outfit" or "what's wrong with that guy." While someone operating from higher consciousness and closer to the frequency of love would say "that person is simply being that person, that has nothing to do with me." Do you see the difference? The very people who judge the guy for his interesting clothing, are probably repressing a part of themselves that fears to be judged. We don't judge anything that doesn't trigger something inside of us. This can mean triggering our belief systems, our conditioning, and more time than not our subconscious. When we judge, energetically we are now entering a different frequency. Subconsciously we are now trying to control another person because what they are doing doesn't align with something we would do or feel comfortable doing. But why does that have anything to do with you? You will not be punished for your judgment, but your judgment will punish you. Not only are you not accepting the universe as it is, you are actually directing negative energy outwards. Now, your energy is emitting judgment and you may be able to guess what happens next. The universe mirrors your judgment! The most judgmental people are those that fear the most to be judged. It's simply a reflection. We project outwards what we feel within, and our projections are what creates our reality, ever so creating energetic matches to the vibratory frequency we are emitting. Tomorrow we will talk about why it's important to get rid of our judgments.

Let's practice those affirmations again! This time, write whatever feels right.

Affirmations

1. _____
2. _____
3. _____
4. _____
5. _____

Post Meditation Reflection: How did your meditation go?

(As well, consider writing a reflection upon judgment as we discussed earlier.)

_____

_____

_____

_____

_____

Let us meet again for Day 19 :)

Day 19

Let's start with 5 things you are grateful for in your life

1. _____

2. _____

3. _____

4. _____

5. _____

Great!

Now let's set an intention for today...

Intention for Day 19

_____

Todays Mental Practice

Throughout the next 60 days there will be a meditation practice for each day. You are now on the second level of our meditation practice and today's meditation will be ten minutes like yesterday. These meditations will get longer as the days go on. Today's theme is abandoning judgment. I believe this to be of utmost importance when in relation to spiritual growth.

"Why should we abandon Judgment?"

Firstly I'd like to note the difference between judgment and discernment. When we talk about abandoning judgment, I don't mean abandoning investigation skills and to not be skeptical as you interact with certain people and places. This isn't what I mean at all. You should always trust your intuition, even whilst reading these excerpts, if something doesn't resonate simply let it go and take what does. This is an important skill to have. To be able to say "nah, that isn't for me." This isn't a judgment, it's a choice. Oftentimes we judge what we don't understand. Judgment is actually the tell tale sign of unconsciousness, while love and openness is a sign of higher consciousness. When we judge, we listen to the opinions of the voice in our head and claim them as ours. Again falling into the trap of residing in our egoic narrative. The reason judgment is such a hindrance to spiritual growth, is because it closes every option of our future being magical. When we live our lives constantly expecting what each moment and day will look like, we leave no room for the unknown. There's no space in our experience for the universe to show us this world is more than you think. Break down that statement, the world is more than you think. Until you allow the world to be as it actually is and not how you think it is, you're going to keep recycling the same experiences in which you've always had. When you drop your judgment and allow the universe to prove to you how crazy and magical this life experience is, your reality transforms. Have you ever met someone you felt like you could just be your complete self around? You can act as silly as you want and they won't judge you and try to tell you how to act. Well this is how the universe feels when you treat life in that manner. The universe can only show you what your perspective and perception allows for. Everything changes when you consciously decide to stop judging. Your life will change, your relationships will change, and your relationship with your higher self will be ignited.

Let's practice those affirmations again! This time, write whatever feels right.

Affirmations

1. _____
2. _____
3. _____
4. _____
5. _____

Post Meditation Reflection: How did your meditation go?

(As well, consider writing a reflection upon judgment as we discussed earlier.)

_____

_____

_____

_____

_____

Let us meet again for Day 20 :)

Day 20

Let's start with 5 things you are grateful for in your life

1. _____
2. _____
3. _____
4. _____
5. _____

Sweet!

Now let's set an intention for today...

Intention for Day 20

_____

Todays Mental Practice

Throughout the next 60 days there will be a meditation practice for each day. You are now on the second level of our meditation practice and today's meditation will be ten minutes like yesterday. These meditations will get longer as the days go on. Today's theme is examining what happens when we actually do abandon judgment. This is fascinating to me because I believe it to be the quickest way to elevate spiritually!

"What happens when we abandon Judgment?"

As noted in yesterday's writing, everything changes. The practice of catching yourself in the midst of judgment and choosing to release that energy with love is immensely powerful. You will see a difference in your life immediately when you rid yourself of judgment. But now it's time to talk about where releasing our judgment becomes the most effective.

The judgment of darkness.

While it is true that one of the main functions of darkness in our life is to show us the value of light, I believe there is a deeper component to this lesson that we can tap into. One of those being us learning to not judge the darkness. That's because we are the ones who assign an experience or an emotion to be dark. The universe itself has no agenda, though there are negative and positive polarities, nothing is inherently good or bad unless decided by conscious beings who have a code of morality in which to assign good and bad. What makes a good or bad experience, is your perspective towards said experience. You and your friend could go ziplining and whilst your friend had the time of their lives, you are maybe scared of heights and had a completely traumatizing experience. So was the experience inherently good or bad? It would depend on who you ask. The experience itself doesn't have any sort of motive, it's just the unfolding of the present. We often look back at some of the darkest moments in our lives and are grateful for them because without them we wouldn't be who we are. But what if we now implement this deeper perspective in real time? What if we can learn to not judge darkness as it is right in front of us? That would actually alter the experience of "dark moments." Now we can understand how powerful we really are. By forging light within us and elevating our awareness we alchemize darkness into light. Suffering into lessons. Lead into gold. So just by abandoning our judgment and allowing room for a greater truth to take hold inside of us we transform the current life we live. We again see oneness and beauty everywhere, realizing that it was always us who decided where to see it and where not to. Duality exists for the sole purpose of learning. In reality, all is one. All are different expressions of the frequency of love, and though in some moments it may feel like that energy is nowhere to be seen, it's always there and we can align with it within ourselves at all times. This is one of the greatest lessons to be learned. This is what is so special about having the opportunity to be a physically conscious being, we can experience the remembering of our true divinity. We can experience light and love, as though it is some otherworldly sensation, only to realize that we are the very spark we have been looking for our whole lives.

Let's practice those affirmations again! This time, write whatever feels right.

Affirmations

1. _____
2. _____
3. _____
4. _____
5. _____

Post Meditation Reflection: How did your meditation go?

(As well, consider writing a reflection upon judgment as we discussed earlier.)

Let us meet again for Day 21 :)

Day 21

Let's start with 5 things you are grateful for in your life

1. _____
2. _____
3. _____
4. _____
5. _____

Nice!

Now let's set an intention for today...

Intention for Day 21

_____

Todays Mental Practice

Throughout the next 60 days there will be a meditation practice for each day. You are now on the second level of our meditation practice and today's meditation will be ten minutes like yesterday. These meditations will get longer as the days go on. Today's theme is understanding how perspective creates reality.

"Why is perspective so important?"

The way we see the world, creates the world we see. This truth holds more power than I think many people realize. In a world of energy and consciousness, all is mental. We shouldn't try to compensate for our lack of fulfillment within us by trying to add more to the world around us. Rather, when we forge a light within and walk the path that starts inside of us, our outer reality will reflect this. So whilst we navigate our inner space, it's important we realize the power many of our belief systems hold over us. Everybody who lives in a state of unconsciousness has strong defense systems around how they see the world. That's because if those beliefs were to be proven incorrect, it would shatter everything they know their lives to be. Soon, if not already, you will find out that the more you learn the more you realize we really don't know. That is why an open perspective is so important. Also when I say we don't know, I simply mean we don't know the whole picture. I know from my experiences what I know to be my truth, but yours may be a bit different, and that's ok. Where there is oneness, there is also the limitless. I believe the truth sometimes may be too hard to comprehend from our current level of consciousness, so the truth takes on many forms in an attempt to guide us back home. Home is within. What you will find is that every profound experience you have is felt inside of you, even if someone or something triggered it, you are still the one producing the chemical reaction in your body and you are also the one making the connections in your life to reveal greater truths. I believe the truth of our nature here in existence is fluid. I believe we are the purpose and our experience here is the why. I believe what we do with this is what creates the truth of our particular life experience. So when you choose to believe something, you hold this divine limitless energy hostage. But when we open ourselves, and allow ourselves to constantly be shown the magic of this universe and allow greater truths to keep revealing themselves, we do ourselves spiritual justice. For our soul is flexible and lucid. Much of what we take to be so serious, was actually meant to be play. For after survival, what else is left but play?

Let's practice those affirmations again! This time, write whatever feels right.

Affirmations

1. _____

2. _____

3. _____

4. _____

5. _____

Post Meditation Reflection: How did your meditation go?

(As well, consider writing a reflection upon perspective as we discussed earlier.)

_____

_____

_____

_____

Let us meet again for Day 22 :)

Day 22

Let's start with 5 things you are grateful for in your life

1. _____
2. _____
3. _____
4. _____
5. _____

Awesome!

Now let's set an intention for today...

Intention for Day 22

_____

Todays Mental Practice

Throughout the next 60 days there will be a meditation practice for each day. You are now on the **Third Level** of our meditation practice and today's meditation will be fifteen minutes! Another five minute jump but I know that you got this! These meditations will get longer as the days go on. Today's theme is compassion and understanding why it's so important.

"Why is compassion so important?"

Oftentimes it takes another person many initiations before they can understand true compassion. This is why we see people of older age to be sometimes more patient and understanding rather than younger people who are still possibly too caught up in the busyness of their daily lives. As well, we see this trait come more naturally to women rather than men. That's because often women mature faster and are more tapped into their emotional side. But for everyone, and especially for younger men, learning compassion at a young age will transform you and allow you to connect at a deeper level with your soul. As well, we often see people who have been through tough times come out the other side significantly more compassionate. One can assume this path they took was needed, for now as a kind individual they can be of great service to the collective. This of course leads us back to oneness. When an individual is tapped into or close to the frequency of love, compassion comes easier. Everything becomes easier when we surrender to love, because love is the highest frequency, it is the original energy before polarity. When we operate from a place of love we see ourselves in other people. We start to not blame people for their anger and prejudices, because maybe for them, this is all part of their path to knowing a greater truth. Many ancient beliefs and traditions believe that this could take many lifetimes and that a person awakening to their truth is just a product of the soul's development. I believe true compassion isn't trying to change anyone but rather loving them exactly the way they are. I believe this to be the most profound way to change someone's life, simply to love them exactly the way they are without needing absolutely anything else from them. This is how you serve, with your love. People will go to great lengths to try and help the people around them without realizing the most powerful way to help them would be to first help yourself. Your love, the energy it holds, spreads to a much greater degree than your words ever can. Then, when your words themselves carry the frequency of love in them, you are of even greater service. When acting in love, you will always be guided to fulfilling your destiny. Always.

Let's practice those affirmations again! This time, write whatever feels right.

Affirmations

1. _____
2. _____
3. _____
4. _____
5. _____

Post Meditation Reflection: How did your meditation go?

(As well, consider writing a reflection upon compassion as we discussed earlier.)

_____

_____

_____

_____

Let us meet again for Day 23 :)

Day 23

Let's start with 5 things you are grateful for in your life

1. _____
2. _____
3. _____
4. _____
5. _____

Awesome!

Now let's set an intention for today...

Intention for Day 23

_____

Todays Mental Practice

Throughout the next 60 days there will be a meditation practice for each day. You are now on the Third Level of our meditation practice and today's meditation will be fifteen minutes. These meditations will get longer as the days go on. Today's theme is self respect. Until we value and respect ourselves as individuals, outer reality will not mirror this back to us.

"Why is self respect so important?"

The exact amount of respect one has for themselves is the exact amount they will tolerate from others. When I say respect, I'm not referencing any sort of appeasement to the ego. Rather I believe respect to be an expression of love. Seeing another person, another soul, on their journey and respecting that. This also includes respecting yourself. Respecting yourself as a person that deserves to be around people that value you, and having enough respect for yourself to leave an environment that is hindering you negatively. Again, all that we have is our relationship with ourselves. Often you will see those that tolerate a significant amount of disrespect from others, also tolerate disrespect from their inner voice. So, someone disrespects you, what now? I'd like you to think of an answer before moving on.

How do we interact with disrespectful people?

Now I'd like you to take your answer and compare it to the bar we talked about earlier. In case you forgot, the quickest way to see if how you're moving forward is in alignment with your highest self just ask yourself a simple question.

How far have I stayed from the frequency of pure love?

Of course no one is perfect and we have moments of lapse, but this is always a question you can come back to for reference. Some might say "that's unreasonable" and to that I say according to who? Who made the rule that humans are naturally violent and reactive? Who made the rule that humans must retaliate instead of act with love? This is unconscious behavior, it fuels our animalistic desire not the desire of our souls. Human beings are evolving spiritually, and this is the way of a being in higher consciousness. Unless of course one needs to defend themselves and those they care about, why would we ever entertain someone who is wanting to bring us into a negative energy, a low vibrational frequency. When walking away is an option, walk away. This is harder said than done, but understand we are all fractions of the same energy, whoever you intend to hurt physically or with your words, you are truly harming yourself. That is why I state the importance of living intentionally with love, or at first at least trying. There is no room for violence in a peaceful world, you are either helping create or helping to bring it down. Love is respect. Give it even if it's not returned. Just as the universe loves you, whether you love it back or not.

Let's practice those affirmations again! This time, write whatever feels right.

Affirmations

1. _____
2. _____
3. _____
4. _____
5. _____

Post Meditation Reflection: How did your meditation go?
(As well, consider writing a reflection upon self respect as we discussed earlier.)

Let us meet again for Day 24 :)

Day 24

Let's start with 5 things you are grateful for in your life

1. _____
2. _____
3. _____
4. _____
5. _____

Nice!

Now let's set an intention for today...

Intention for Day 24

_____

Todays Mental Practice

Throughout the next 60 days there will be a meditation practice for each day. You are now on the Third Level of our meditation practice and today's meditation will be fifteen minutes. These meditations will get longer as the days go on. Today's theme is solitude.

"Why is solitude so important?"

The first thing I want to address in regards to this topic is balance. Too much alone time isn't helpful in my opinion and likewise not enough alone time can be detrimental as well. We are social creatures physically and our souls crave connection. Remember to take oneness into account, other people are extensions of the same energy. That's why being with those of similar energy as you is so helpful, it elevates everyone involved into new heights and realizations. Now that we got that out of the way, let's dive into why time alone can be extremely helpful. Most people are a product of their environment. This isn't a bad thing, even the sense of humor you share with your friends is attributed to where you're from and how you surround yourself. But what happens when we get no alone time is that our energy begins to lose its authenticity. When we get no alone time our energy starts to merge with those we've been around all the time. Even if it's just an hour out of your day, take some time to recharge and come into your space. Meditation helps with this because it takes us out of all these beliefs and narratives that have influenced our energy field. Unconsciously we literally become who we surround ourselves with, even the way you speak, act, and eat are all influenced by those around you if you're always immersed in sociality. So what happens when we take some real time to ourselves? We become more of who we are. Sometimes people need a complete reset because they haven't had alone time in so long. If this is necessary, let it be so. But for most, it's simply a practice of balance. By nature we are afraid to be alone. When we lived in the wild, this meant danger. But we are moving past our animal instincts in exchange for a more soul aligned life. Solitude will only bring you temporary peace, you must learn to forge this peace even amongst the chaos of life. This way of building resilience is sustainable. We should want to be able to be attuned to our highest state of being no matter where we are. This, within reason of course, but I invite you to investigate beliefs that are hindering you from living as so. (Ex: "I can only be at peace if I get a cabin in the woods.")

Let's practice those affirmations again! This time, write whatever feels right.

Affirmations

1. _____
2. _____
3. _____
4. _____
5. _____

Post Meditation Reflection: How did your meditation go?

(As well, consider writing a reflection upon solitude as we discussed earlier.)

_____

_____

_____

_____

_____

Let us meet again for Day 25 :)

Day 25

Let's start with 5 things you are grateful for in your life

1. _____
2. _____
3. _____
4. _____
5. _____

Sweet!

Now let's set an intention for today...

Intention for Day 25

Todays Mental Practice

Throughout the next 60 days there will be a meditation practice for each day. You are now on the Third Level of our meditation practice and today's meditation will be fifteen minutes. These meditations will get longer as the days go on. Today's theme will be investigating what exactly the ego is, and how we develop a healthy relationship with it through understanding its purpose.

"What is Ego?"

Firstly, ego is your sense of human self. It is the labels that have been assigned to you and that you have assigned to yourself in this lifetime. Examples are your name, your job/school, where you live, who you're friends with. These are all things that you possess in a way, but those things can be stripped to reveal more. So no, ego is not bad, but it's also not good. It just is. When one would say "he has a big ego" that would mean he is very in love with his false sense of self. He takes great pride in the things mentioned before. Also could be good or bad, it really just depends. So the trick here is creating a balance of appreciating ego and respecting it for what it is, but also knowing that it doesn't cover the full spectrum of your beingness. This isn't meant to damage your perception of who you are, but rather challenge you to see who you are beyond ego when there is no one to perform for and no one to impress. This also challenges you to love said ego, and cultivate it in a way where it aligns more with the truest representation of you. The desire to kill the ego, is the work of ego.

How can we recognize when our ego is at work?

This is a valid question we can ask ourselves during our daily lives. Traits of ego led action often portrays traits that may appear defensive or possessive. The ego's whole thing is that it wishes to control. But just because the ego wishes for something doesn't mean that's where it will thrive. Ego thrives as a sort of filter we carry with us through our life. We know ego to simply be a means by which our souls can experience reality. This also brings us to why ego isn't inherently bad. When an individual is self realized and knows themselves to be beyond ego, they can then form a healthy and thriving relationship between soul and ego. They value things that the ego does, but at the same time do not weigh their worth based on these things. Let us say someone would like to treat themselves to a piece of clothing they enjoy. Any type of reaction to this process that takes place on either end of the spectrum of polarity would be the process of ego. This nice piece of clothing satisfies the ego but yet does not diminish the energy of the soul unless you allow it to do so. The assumption that you must not be successful in this material world to be "spiritual" is the work of ego. Then on the other side, the assumption that you are only worthy if you are successful in the material world is also the work of ego. See past belief systems, and see that neutrality exists all around us and it is our perception that creates our reality. Balance is necessary, always.

Let's practice those affirmations again! This time, write whatever feels right.

Affirmations

1. _____
2. _____
3. _____
4. _____
5. _____

Post Meditation Reflection: How did your meditation go?

(As well, consider writing a reflection upon the ego as we discussed earlier.)

_____

_____

Let us meet again for Day 26 :)

Day 26

Let's start with 5 things you are grateful for in your life

1. _____
2. _____
3. _____
4. _____
5. _____

Great!

Now let's set an intention for today...

Intention for Day 26

_____

Todays Mental Practice

Throughout the next 60 days there will be a meditation practice for each day. You are now on the Third Level of our meditation practice and today's meditation will be fifteen minutes. These meditations will get longer as the days go on. Today's theme will be similar to yesterdays but with a little twist. Investigating the new found spiritual ego!

"What is spiritual Ego?"

The spiritual ego is a sneaky mechanism our ego uses that often goes under the radar. Especially nowadays there are many people who consider themselves to be "spiritual." But this is a broad term because there is no such thing as being more spiritual than another person. We are all spirits, any act of ours can be considered spiritual. Sometimes people will believe themselves to be better than others because of the knowledge they have attained. They may find normal conversations mundane, and see those who are "awakened" to be of more importance than those who are "asleep." Never forget that we are one, no one is better than anyone else, no one is worth more than another person. I'd like us to examine the narrative of someone who says certain activities are less "spiritual" and those who do those activities are less spiritual as well. My question has always been: what rules do you garner this belief from? There is no rulebook to this thing we call life, actually far from it. Our perception is literally what creates the limitations of our life experience. So it would possibly be more appropriate to say that another person is more limited rather than less spiritual. This would only work because openness is the foundation to elevation in consciousness and awareness. The less one is attached to their belief systems and their individual narrative of reality the more space they create for new perspectives. Often it is our belief of a certain thing that is more harmful than the thing itself. "I can't have a nice car and be spiritual", "I can't go out with my friends and be spiritual", "I can't live in a certain place and be spiritual." Where are these rules and limitations coming from? Certainly not from the universe! The universe is a flowing consciousness of unconditional love and support. Do you know what this means? It loves and supports you no matter what, and that is because you are one with it. Any rules you believe this life to have in terms of how you must live your life have been self imposed. The reason you are always right where you need to be is because you are limitless. Your higher self is like a grand architect guiding you in the direction to keep understanding the greatest truth: everything is within you already. You create a more loving and peaceful world not by judging others for their actions but by you yourself becoming more loving and peaceful. Every individual, like you, is a piece of the one. They too are limitless and are co creators of their realities. They too are being guided by their higher selves. All you can ever do is inspire change in others through setting an example in yourself. There is no one and nothing else to control except for your own beingness. Each person is on their own journey, and you do more harm than good trying to "wake them up." Everybody is already awake, but chose to come here and dream, so let everyone experience this life in a way that their souls provide. If they need you to be their spark, it will happen without you even knowing you helped them. Loosen your grasp of your opinions on this world, and allow your first step to be love always.

Let's practice those affirmations again! This time, write whatever feels right.

Affirmations

1. _____
2. _____
3. _____
4. _____
5. _____

Post Meditation Reflection: How did your meditation go?

(As well, consider writing a reflection upon the spiritual ego as we discussed earlier.)

_____

_____

_____

_____

_____

_____

_____

Let us meet again for Day 27 :)

Day 27

Let's start with 5 things you are grateful for in your life

1. _____

2. _____

3. _____

4. _____

5. _____

Sweet!

Now let's set an intention for today...

Intention for Day 27

_____

Todays Mental Practice

Throughout the next 60 days there will be a meditation practice for each day. You are now on the Third Level of our meditation practice and today's meditation will be fifteen minutes. These meditations will get longer as the days go on. Today's theme is understanding reflections.

"What does understanding reflections mean?"

If you haven't yet figured it out, reality is simply a mirror to the relationship you have with yourself. How you feel within sends out a unique energetic frequency into the universe and your reality is a series of events in which things that closely match your energetic frequency will be drawn towards you. The universe treats you, exactly how you treat you. That is because you are the universe, and there is only ever the universe experiencing itself. So though we call it a mirror, there really is only one relationship ever happening. Take this as an example. When you start meditating a lot, your relationship with your thoughts completely changes. Let's say you have finally reached a point where you don't judge your thoughts, no matter how ridiculous, no matter how frightening, no matter how out of character these thoughts seem, you sit there and accept them. You don't judge them, you allow them in, and you love them. For you know your reaction to thoughts is what dictates your future, not the thoughts themselves. Now a person who practices this, will often appear to others as a very non judgmental person. People will feel like they can be fully themselves around this person and don't have to worry about being judged and ridiculed. This is because of the reflection of this person treating themselves in this manner. The person may not even realize they are creating such a welcoming environment for others, but nonetheless it is felt in the hearts of those they spend time with. In the same way, someone who is very harsh and judgemental of themselves, will create this sort of environment for others within their energy. The only relationship you ever really have is with yourself. Because the only relationship that exists is the universe's relationship with itself. You are both infinite and limitless, experiencing what it is like to forget you are so. Whatever you seek to create for others, you must create within yourself. You can only create a more peaceful and loving world by becoming more peaceful and loving. Your energy will be of service to the degree your words cannot.

Let's practice those affirmations again! This time, write whatever feels right.

Affirmations

1. _____
2. _____
3. _____
4. _____
5. _____

Post Meditation Reflection: How did your meditation go?

(As well, consider writing a reflection upon reflections as we discussed earlier.)

_____

_____

_____

_____

_____

Let us meet again for Day 28 :)

Day 28

Let's start with 5 things you are grateful for in your life

1. _____
2. _____
3. _____
4. _____
5. _____

Nice!

Now let's set an intention for today...

Intention for Day 28

_____

Todays Mental Practice

Throughout the next 60 days there will be a meditation practice for each day. You are now on the Third Level of our meditation practice and today's meditation will be fifteen minutes. These meditations will get longer as the days go on. Today's theme is breaking down the idea that the universe is "testing" us.

"Is the universe testing you?"

Well, yes and no. Is there an intelligence beyond you moving things in your direction for your spiritual growth? Yes. Is this intelligence also you? Yes. There is an intricate relationship between you and your higher self. Any "test" you may encounter is called forth by you. Either consciously or unconsciously. As well, the only reason it would ever be considered a test is if you believed it to be so. Your higher self is constantly trying to show you that all your power is within. It will go to great lengths to keep reminding you of this. Your perception and beliefs is what creates your reality, and until you are conscious of this, sure there will be many tests. The answer is always you are whole and perfect just the way you are. You are worthy of love, paradise, and prosperity. The only tests you will receive will be in an attempt to break any sort of belief that stands in the way of you believing you are deserving of these things. One may ask "if my higher self is orchestrating everything, do I even have free will?" Yes, you have free will to the highest degree that you can imagine. But if we are talking from a ground level, it can appear to be that you do not. Destiny is the free will of the higher self. But if we can come into alignment with the frequency of our highest self (love) we can see that everything we wanted our destiny to be, it already is. It's simply a matter of becoming conscious. When we become conscious, we become aware of the lessons, we become aware of the limiting beliefs we are still holding. Things will go more smoothly not by us trying to control our future, but by us coming into the frequency of ourselves that already has control. This is actually a paradox, because once we come into alignment with a higher frequency, love or our higher self whichever way you want to look at, we actually do not desire control! We are so in tune with ourselves and our faith, that the present moment is the only thing we ever pay our attention to. We have unwavering faith that we are the creator of our reality. We have complete trust in our higher self, because we have now become our higher self, and the decisions we make from that frequency are the same decisions our higher self has made for us in the physical. Now remember, there is no becoming your highest self there is only realizing that you already are. It's about clearing the way and letting ourselves soften enough to find our way home, not about chasing some feeling we believe to be attained. There is no destination, there is only realization.

Let's practice those affirmations again! This time, write whatever feels right.

Affirmations

1. _____
2. _____
3. _____
4. _____
5. _____

Post Meditation Reflection: How did your meditation go?

(As well, consider writing a reflection upon "tests" as we discussed earlier.)

_____

_____

_____

Let us meet again for Day 29 :)

Day 29

Let's start with 5 things you are grateful for in your life

1. _____

2. _____

3. _____

4. _____

5. _____

Sweet!

Now let's set an intention for today...

Intention for Day 29

Todays Mental Practice

Throughout the next 60 days there will be a meditation practice for each day. You are now on the Third Level of our meditation practice and today's meditation will be fifteen minutes. These meditations will get longer as the days go on. Today's theme is authenticity and examining why it is so important to be ourselves.

"Why is authenticity so important?"

When you are truly yourself, you will align with the things that you truly want in this life. We know already that every person emits an energetic frequency that is unique to them. We may see overlapping emotions in this energy being emitted based on how the person feels most of the time. If a person lives their lives with a lot of fear, this emotion carries significant weight in the unique frequency this person is projecting. Here's the bottom line, until you take responsibility for how you feel within, it won't be easy to change your life. Until you stop allowing the situations of your life to determine how you feel, you will remain being the victim of your life rather than the creator of it. Life is a wonky ride, but we always have a choice of how we react to any given situation. The sooner you accept full responsibility, the sooner you can begin the process of alchemizing the darkness within you into light. A better way of saying this may be the process of bringing what is dark within you to light. This way of connecting with ourselves and discovering who we truly are past the fear, trauma, and anxiety will allow us to gain better control of the energy we project onto the world. Many people get caught in this trap of not wanting to "pretend" to be someone they are not. But who are you really? If you've lived much of your life from a state of unconsciousness, can you truly say you have been your most authentic self? Anyway, the self as we know it is very much illusory. You can go across the world and act like a different person and no one would bat an eye. That's because you're limiting yourself to fitting into the narrative of who you've always been. You are keeping up this sort of act to fit the character of who your friends and family know you to be. Are we not allowed to change? You may realize you're following a set of unspoken conditions and rules without even knowing it. Once awareness has been met, our energy changes immediately. As soon as you start to think, "there are no rules, I can change," your energy field opens up and becomes less stagnant than it was before. That's because our level of consciousness also affects our energy, and as you continue to walk the path of self discovery and realization you will see there is simply no point to not being yourself, for that is what you came here to do. Be one with your energy and love yourself for it. Allow all people and future experiences to meet you at this frequency.

Let's practice those affirmations again! This time, write whatever feels right.

Affirmations

1. _____
2. _____
3. _____
4. _____
5. _____

Post Meditation Reflection: How did your meditation go?

(As well, consider writing a reflection upon authenticity as we discussed earlier.)

_____

_____

_____

Let us meet again for Day 30 :)

Day 30

You are officially half way through your journey. I can only imagine it's been a hell of a ride thus far. Today, we're going to do something different. We are going to practice shadow work. First we will talk about why it is important to love your shadow and second you will answer some questions for you to reflect upon in relation to loving your shadow.

"How do we love our shadow?"

As your light grows, you will notice a shadow within your sights. This shadow may try to pull you back into old habits when things get tough. You may be inclined to neglect this shadow and ignore it as something outside of you. But this does not tame the shadow, and in many cases it makes it grow larger. Life is not simply a process of knowing light, it is also a process of learning darkness. This may sound scary, but I promise whatever conceptions you have about your darkness and whatever it is within you that you feel you are ignoring is much scarier in your thoughts than in reality. In truth, life is about balancing light and dark, with our intention in service to the light, whilst also opening our hearts to the dark. Light needs darkness to exist, just as many of us need catalysts in our life to evolve. Oftentimes we look back at some of the darkest moments in our lives and realize we needed to be there and feel those emotions to become who we are today. Understand that without the darkness you have felt, you would have never been inspired to change, to awaken.

How do we love our shadow?

In the same way we practice not judging our negative thoughts, we must also not judge our shadow. Within the universe inside of you, you are the higher power. To the cells, bones, and all the organs in your body, they rely on you. Within this universe also lies that of the mind, the mind creates the shadow. You can imagine this as a physical description, our immense light shines bright, but this causes a shadow in physical reality. The only way to ease the cries and desperations of the shadow, is not to turn our back towards it but instead face it. We accept it as part of us, and we show it our love. What happens is the shadow was never really just a shadow in the first place. After you face it, your light reveals what's been hiding within the darkness of the shadow all along. It's you, as a child.

Some questions for understanding our shadow!

What is the first word you associate with your childhood?

What is one moment from your past you felt betrayed or abandoned?

Do you see any correlation between what you struggle with now and what you struggled with when you were younger?

_____

_____

What parts of yourself do you think you are ashamed of?

_____

_____

I'd like you to imagine yourself as a child, really picture it in your head. Now off intuition alone, what is the first thing a child says to you? (Don't overthink it, whatever comes to you first just write it down.)

_____

_____

_____

Now I'd like you to affirm this message with me outloud.

"I accept and love all parts of myself. I invite any part of myself that feels neglected or unloved to make itself known in my awareness. I understand that through the frequency of love, I can heal and nurture my inner child. Any darkness within me is illuminated by my love. I am that I am, and that is enough."

Great work, I know that might've been a little bit difficult. The reason I ask you to affirm this message out loud is because words carry energy, and when that energy is matched with intention, healing can take initiative. More on this in tomorrow's reading.

As well, you are now on the fourth level of our meditation practice! I now invite you to challenge yourself and up that daily meditation number to 20 minutes! Remember, any meditation is better than no meditation. Even if you feel the traffic of the thoughts are overwhelming, sit in the storm, and build your resilience, it will be more than worth it.

Post Meditation Reflection: How did your meditation go?
(As well, consider writing a reflection upon shadow work as we discussed earlier.)

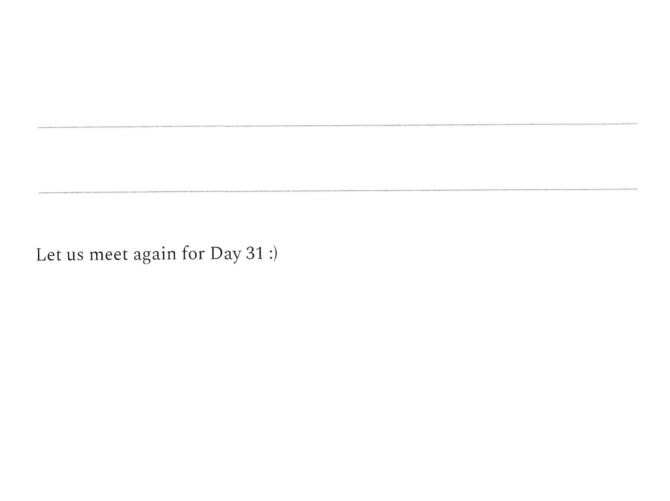

Let us meet again for Day 31 :)

Day 31

Let's start with 5 things you are grateful for in your life

1. _____
2. _____
3. _____
4. _____
5. _____

Great!

Now let's set an intention for today...

Intention for Day 31

_____

Todays Mental Practice

Throughout the next 60 days there will be a meditation practice for each day. You are now on the Fourth Level of our meditation practice and today's meditation will be twenty minutes. These meditations will get longer as the days go on. Today's theme is examining how our words carry energy.

"How do words carry energy?"

Everything in this world holds energy, words especially. The words you speak affect your life in two ways. The first being the way it affects your subconscious. Your mind, like said before, behaves in many ways like a computer. It takes the words it hears and the emotions it experiences and from there formulates how our unconscious will behave. A couple things to note, our unconscious doesn't know the difference between an imagined reality and a real one. Our minds operate solely based on how we feel and think and it uses that to assess if an experience is real. That's why when you're daydreaming about someone you like, you actually feel the emotions as if it were real. Your brain knows this to be real within the paradigm that it operates in. So you can imagine the day dreaming or should we say day worrying of unfortunate and scary events also leaves its mark on our unconscious mind. As well, the unconscious mind is limited. It doesn't know when you are talking about yourself or another person. When an individual is constantly speaking negatively upon others, it's not surprising when that same individual deals with insecurity and worrying about what others think. Their mind is conditioned to judge negatively. Whether that be their own self or others. So you must be mindful in the way in which you speak. Don't carry this principle with too much weight though, for obsessing over the words you speak may act as just another attachment. Nothing is ever worth obsessing over, and frankly your attachment to any given teaching can be more harmful than the benefit you gain from the teaching itself. So be mindful when speaking, but don't self analyze your way into more problems than you need to. You'll notice as you become conscious of the words you speak and make an effort to speak more positively about yourself and others that your brain naturally starts to become more positive with the thoughts it provides for you. The second way words affect your life is the actual energy they carry within themselves. Be mindful of your intention when speaking, for words carry this energy signature with them and act as a projection of your own energy into the universe. Just like any projection we create with our energy, it will mirror itself back to us.

Let's practice those affirmations again! This time, write whatever feels right.

Affirmations

1. _____
2. _____
3. _____
4. _____
5. _____

Post Meditation Reflection: How did your meditation go?

(As well, consider writing a reflection upon the power of words as we discussed earlier.)

_____

_____

_____

_____

Let us meet again for Day 32 :)

Day 32

Let's start with 5 things you are grateful for in your life

1. _____
2. _____
3. _____
4. _____
5. _____

Awesome!

Now let's set an intention for today...

Intention for Day 32

_____

Todays Mental Practice

Throughout the next 60 days there will be a meditation practice for each day. You are now on the Fourth Level of our meditation practice and today's meditation will be twenty minutes. These meditations will get longer as the days go on. Today's theme is learning to understand and respect every other person's journey.

"The journey of others."

Naturally, once you start improving and evolving physically and spiritually, you'll want your friends and family to join in on the fun. You may go to great lengths to "wake them up" and try to lead them down what you believe to be a more fulfilling life. This, as you would've learned on your own as well, has consequences. When we try to impose our will on the freedom of others, we are now not acting from our soul, we are acting from our ego. It is not your job to awaken anyone, if you were looking for a way to awaken the most amount of people possible, guess what you do? You love them, and you embody the teachings you wish to share with them. A fundamental law that I have noticed is that you can not impede on someone elses free will. This creates a great amount of resistance and goes completely against the flow of life. The most divine and serviceful thing you can ever do to help the people around you is let them be who they are and love them without conditions. The assumption that another person is "asleep" is really just our ego trying to create another way to instill a power dynamic. No one is better than anyone else because we are all the same consciousness! This does not mean ignoring the people struggling around you. Be there for them and listen to them. Your friend who is going through a tough time probably isn't looking for a spiritual awakening, they are just looking for someone to care. Being spiritual doesn't make you an inherently good person, being kind and loving towards others makes you a good person. Do not abandon your personhood, you have infinite time to do that, but you only have a limited time being the person you are now. Do not allow your understanding of deeper truths to make you grow cold, instead allow them to show you how you can appreciate more things and people than you did before. Let your wisdom guide you to deeper love, and allow your deeper love to transform your life effortlessly.

Let's practice those affirmations again! This time, write whatever feels right.

Affirmations

1. _____
2. _____
3. _____
4. _____
5. _____

Post Meditation Reflection: How did your meditation go?

(As well, consider writing a reflection upon the journey of others as we discussed earlier.)

_____

_____

_____

_____

_____

_____

Let us meet again for Day 33 :)

Day 33

Let's start with 5 things you are grateful for in your life

1. _____
2. _____
3. _____
4. _____
5. _____

Perfect!

Now let's set an intention for today...

Intention for Day 33

_____

Todays Mental Practice

Throughout the next 60 days there will be a meditation practice for each day. You are now on the Fourth Level of our meditation practice and today's meditation will be twenty minutes. These meditations will get longer as the days go on. Today's theme is learning to dance amongst the storm;)

"How do we lighten up?"

The more I try to investigate the seriousness of this reality and the seriousness of the path all of us wish to walk, the more I realize nothing is that serious. The birds that sing outside don't seem to be too serious, the sunset I watch in awe doesn't seem to be too serious, whenever I feel the most in alignment I never catch myself being very serious. So I don't believe anything to be as serious as we want to make it. Well actually, that's the fun part about the whole thing, is that everything is as serious as we wish to make it. I'd like to use this example: you gather weekly to play soccer with your friends. Everyone takes this weekly matchup very seriously for it's a good way to get some exercise in and fuel that competitive spirit many of us long for. Now what happens when someone gets too competitive and is a bad sport? They get lost in the intensity of the game and they forget everyone is playing for fun. They forget that everyone here made an effort to show up, a group of people came together, and though some are on opposing sides, they still must collaborate to compete. So being too caught up in the trivial things in our lives is like getting lost in the moment but constantly. When you don't remind yourself of the big picture, two things happen. You get lost in the smaller picture and as well you allow yourself to only experience reality at a more shallow level that you could've if you just zoomed out a bit. See the absurd orchestration that is life. See that even beyond all the chaos going on, there is so much collaboration and unity still at work. Everyday you get in the car and you trust your fellow beings to drive safely. Do accidents happen? Sure, but most of the time they dont. Allowing all the little things in your life to weigh you down is like only focusing on the accidents that happen on the road. The key to lightening up is zooming out. Seeing that all this matters, because we are giving it our participation. Now when we carry this perspective with us and still choose to participate is where having fun and being in alignment comes to fruition. Like playing a soccer game and realizing all of it is possible because people came together to do what? To have fun. Does anything have meaning? Yes and no. Both answers are correct and incorrect. That's what makes this reality such an adventure. The way you choose to see the world, creates the world you see. It's about changing perspectives, not changing lives. Lightening up doesn't mean not caring, it means remaining grounded and consciously choosing the way in which we want to experience reality. Choice is the ultimate freedom.

Let's practice those affirmations again! This time, write whatever feels right.

Affirmations

1. _____
2. _____
3. _____
4. _____
5. _____

Post Meditation Reflection: How did your meditation go?

(As well, consider writing a reflection upon lightening up as we discussed earlier.)

_____

_____

_____

Let us meet again for Day 34 :)

Day 34

Let's start with 5 things you are grateful for in your life

1. _____
2. _____
3. _____
4. _____
5. _____

Awesome!

Now let's set an intention for today...

Intention for Day 34

_____

Todays Mental Practice

Throughout the next 60 days there will be a meditation practice for each day. You are now on the Fourth Level of our meditation practice and today's meditation will be twenty minutes. These meditations will get longer as the days go on. Today's theme as well as tommorows theme will be examining if we are living in repeated cycles or if we are evolving.

"What does repeated cycles mean?"

In each of our lives, everyday, we are presented with choices. How we act upon those choices creates a ripple effect in the universe. For each choice, each action holds a vibratory energy. These many actions you take that are embedded with your energetic signature help in the creation of what you know to be your future. This is why being mindful and conscious are once again of great importance. When you continue to make choices in an attempt to ease your internal struggle, this is what we call a repeated cycle. A repeated cycle could be seen as a lesson, but really it's just our external reality reflecting back to us our own unwillingness to let go of energy stuck within us. Like we talked about previously, emotion is energy in motion, and this energy does not like to be stagnant. So when we hold on to fear, anxiety, resentment, etc and we continue to let these emotions dictate our decisions it creates a repeated cycle. This could also be the case with positive emotion but it's extremely rare. When we feel good we don't avoid the world, we open ourselves to it. When we feel bad we close ourselves off to the world, retreating back into old habits. This process of feeling negative and retreating back into our closed inner environment when triggered by a choice to make is what creates repeated cycles. You need to stop making decisions out of the emotions you are trying to let go of. You say that you are ready to evolve past these negative feelings but yet you continue to let them steer the direction of your life. You need to be brave, and understand that running towards the storm will allow you to be out of the storm quicker than if you ran from it. Do it scared, do it anxious, do things because you want to and not because you're trying to avoid the negative feelings you deal with. As well, you will start to build a resilience to the negative emotions and in due time the grasp that this negativity has on you will loosen. This is how you break the cycle.

Let's practice those affirmations again! This time, write whatever feels right.

Affirmations

1. _____
2. _____
3. _____
4. _____
5. _____

Post Meditation Reflection: How did your meditation go?

(As well, consider writing a reflection upon repeated cycles as we discussed earlier.)

_____

_____

_____

_____

_____

_____

Let us meet again for Day 35 :)

Day 35

Let's start with 5 things you are grateful for in your life

1. _____
2. _____
3. _____
4. _____
5. _____

Awesome!

Now let's set an intention for today...

Intention for Day 35

_____

Todays Mental Practice

Throughout the next 60 days there will be a meditation practice for each day. You are now on the Fourth Level of our meditation practice and today's meditation will be twenty minutes. These meditations will get longer as the days go on. Today's theme is understanding what it looks like when we break the repeated cycles we talked about earlier.

"What does it look like to break free?"

How do you know when a repeated cycle has been broken? Well, it can be hard to tell for sure. Most of us will deal with many of the same cycles in our lives, it plays an instrumental part of what our soul needs to learn and experience to evolve. But, you will know when you have made great progress because you pretty much forget about it completely. I bet in yesterday's reading many of you had an emotion you struggle with come to mind when examining the process of repeated cycles. Well, that's part of the cycle as well. I'd like to stress the fact that these repeated cycles aren't bad and the very fact that you're aware enough to notice them in place and are willing to do what you can to let go is a huge positive. Some people will go their whole lives living in the midst of a repeated cycle. Having the simple awareness to note that the cycle is there means the most difficult part is over. The awareness and willingness to want to heal and be better changes your energy already. But if you are still in the process of breaking one of these cycles you'll know you have really broken free when the negative emotion you dealt with for the longest time no longer plays a role in your decision making. It is no longer a factor. Let's say someone had a fear of planes, they would know they have made significant progress when their fear is now merely an afterthought. The key here in breaking free of cycles is once you get over that immediate intense emotion it's a process of seeing things as objectively as you can. This is what it looks like when we operate from a place of higher awareness. You notice the emotion, you notice how it feels in your body and you notice how it affects your thought process. You see it, you label it, and you move forward. Feeling the emotion in all the ways you must, but not letting that emotion dictate your choices. Be patient with yourself, this is your work, this is exactly what you need to guide yourself through to evolve. There's a reason for the things we go through in this life, and we find this reason by loving ourselves enough to stay consistent and realize we deserve better for ourselves then to suffer. You will and must always be your own hero. You will have yourself to thank at the end of the day, always.

Let's practice those affirmations again! This time, write whatever feels right.

Affirmations

1. _____

2. _____

3. _____

4. _____

5. _____

Post Meditation Reflection: How did your meditation go?

(As well, consider writing a reflection upon breaking free as we discussed earlier.)

_____

_____

_____

_____

Let us meet again for Day 36 :)

Day 36

Let's start with 5 things you are grateful for in your life

1. _____
2. _____
3. _____
4. _____
5. _____

Great!

Now let's set an intention for today...

Intention for Day 36

_____

Todays Mental Practice

Throughout the next 60 days there will be a meditation practice for each day. You are now on the Fourth Level of our meditation practice and today's meditation will be twenty minutes. These meditations will get longer as the days go on. Today's theme is the process of healing a broken heart...

"How does one heal a broken heart?"

A broken heart can be very difficult and it can happen for a variety of different reasons. The key to a healthy healing process is a combination of allowing ourselves to feel while also maintaining self responsibility. You have to be open and honest with yourself about how you feel. If the heart is broken from a relationship, it's ok to feel a certain way for that person as long as you need to, but the real work comes in how you act upon these feelings. Just as you don't want to make decisions from fear or anxiety, you also don't want to make decisions from the frequency of your heartbreak. Emotional maturity is allowing yourself to feel all the emotions you need to whilst also moving forward in a more level headed manner. Again, you need to zoom out. When we are hurt by someone who played a big part in our lives it can feel like there is a gap that needs filling. But the last thing you want to do is search for something to fill that gap. Anything you attempt to fill it with will be a temporary fix and not an actual release of the energy you've been holding onto. You need to love yourself, respect yourself, and honor yourself. Even if what the person did to you was wrong, this is about moving on with our lives not revenge. For as long as you are living your life with the motivation of making another person feel some type of way, you will be ruled by this person. Unconsciously every decision you make is in an attempt to further make this person regret what they did to you. Is that really the alignment you wish to come into? Your soul does not hold grudges, so for long as you do, you can not come into your highest alignment. Instead, take the more difficult yet rewarding route and allow this situation to be a trigger towards further self realization and improvement. Don't go looking to fill that gap, that gap has a specific hole that only a certain thing or person can fill. Move on, heal, the gap will disappear in due time. Allow what has been done to you to teach you what not to do to others. You need to release the tension, you need to let go of the need for things to be as they once were. If you hang on to how things once were, you'll never get to see how good things can be.

Let's practice those affirmations again! This time, write whatever feels right.

Affirmations

1. _____
2. _____
3. _____
4. _____
5. _____

Post Meditation Reflection: How did your meditation go?

(As well, consider writing a reflection upon healing a broken heart as we discussed earlier.)

_____

_____

_____

_____

_____

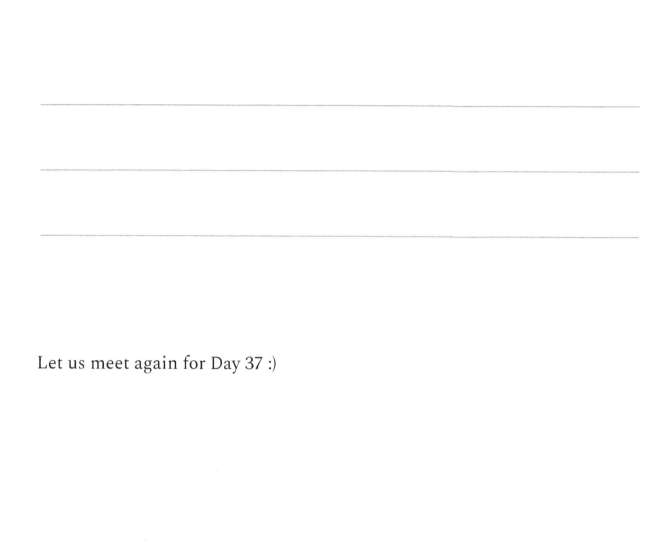

Let us meet again for Day 37 :)

Day 37

Let's start with 5 things you are grateful for in your life

1. _____

2. _____

3. _____

4. _____

5. _____

Sweet!

Now let's set an intention for today...

Intention for Day 37

_____

Todays Mental Practice

Throughout the next 60 days there will be a meditation practice for each day. You are now on the Fourth Level of our meditation practice and today's meditation will be twenty minutes. These meditations will get longer as the days go on. Today's theme is stillness and examining how it can massively benefit our lives.

"How can stillness help us?"

Being still is hard to even call a practice. Watch how your body and your mind react to stillness and this will teach you very much about why the things in your life are the way they are. Stillness of mind or flow state as many refer to it is as close as you can get to a superpower. But what about simple stillness and all its applications. Even with our actions, stillness can be a great beneficiary to the way we make choices in our lives. Many of us feel as if we must always be doing something, always being involved in some sort of activity. But why? This is where the term work smarter not harder really comes into effect. There will be situations such as jobs in which this practice is not applicable but I invite you to practice stillness in the framework of your hobbies or even your social interactions. When we are ok and satisfied being on our own, not having to constantly do something to fulfill us, this leaves room for other things to fulfill us. This can be felt energetically as well. When we practice stillness, suddenly the things we do partake in are all the more powerful. This is because our attention and energy is more potent. It's similar to if you don't get to see someone that often, but when you do see them it's really special. The same things happen with our attention and energy. When we stop dispersing our attention in a million different places and really practice just being here and now not doing anything, it makes our energy more potent. Oftentimes we see people partaking in an activity whilst also thinking about a future activity, whilst also on phone talking about a prior activity. In this case your energy is all over the place, and really each thing you're doing isn't getting the appropriate amount of energy to fully blossom. Consider all the things in your life like plants. The more you water each plant, the more it will grow. But you only have a limited amount of water. Stillness is comparable to letting the water from the sink fully fill up our jug before pouring the water into the plants. Water the plants of your life carefully. Stillness is a state of allowing, it allows us to let go and let what will be, be just that. Ironically, the universe loves space to operate. So when we give it that, it allows for more room for magic to happen. We need to curate a balance of intention and allowing, this is what creates alignment.

Let's practice those affirmations again! This time, write whatever feels right.

Affirmations

1. _____
2. _____
3. _____
4. _____
5. _____

Post Meditation Reflection: How did your meditation go?

(As well, consider writing a reflection upon stillness as we discussed earlier.)

_____

_____

_____

Let us meet again for Day 38 :)

Day 38

Let's start with 5 things you are grateful for in your life

1. _____
2. _____
3. _____
4. _____
5. _____

Awesome!

Now let's set an intention for today...

Intention for Day 38

_____

Todays Mental Practice

Throughout the next 60 days there will be a meditation practice for each day. You are now on the Fourth Level of our meditation practice and today's meditation will be twenty minutes. These meditations will get longer as the days go on. Today's theme is owning your power and not letting past conditioning make you feel guilty for healing.

"How do we own our power?"

To someone who has been timid and quiet their whole life, being confident and sure of themselves may feel unnatural. It actually may feel as if they are being aggressive and demanding, when in reality they are simply finally coming into their power. In the same way, someone who has had trouble controlling their anger in the past may feel as if they are weak for being more kind and patient. The reason these false narratives come into the picture when we start healing is because it's our unconscious defense mechanisms trying to do their job. We've been so used to playing a character our whole lives, and especially if we've been playing this character not authentically, our subconscious will be confused. This is why there is so much resistance that happens inside of you when you start changing for the better. This resistance isn't the universe trying to humble you into going back into the character you once were, it's rather your inner shadow attempting to survive. Again, the inner shadow is merely a protection for our inner child. This inner child projects itself into the issues we feel as we get older. If our inner child was scared of being seen because they were worried they would get judged and bullied, these sensations may come up as you try to own your power with confidence. The universe is working for you. There is no supreme judge that is attempting to balance the scales of all the good things that happen to you with bad things. You are supposed to be prosperous, that is the evolution of consciousness in humans. After survival needs have been met, we are allowed space to navigate our soul's journey. We are given space to be creative and tune into our higher power within us. This is the natural progression of a soul. Nothing is by coincidence, if you are opening your eyes and wanting to heal and align with your soul's purpose don't be surprised by the resistance that comes from owning your power. This could mean falling out of alignment with friends, places, and activities. For long as you are moving forward from a place of love and are acting on your highest excitement and passions you can rest assured you are on the path of least resistance. The universe is not trying to humble you, especially if you are aware of such a mechanism at play. The universe is supporting you in anything you do, it's simply waiting for you to acknowledge that you are one with the universe and you have all the power you need. You gain your power by loving yourself enough to allow things to go well and even expect things to work in your favor.

Let's practice those affirmations again! This time, write whatever feels right.

Affirmations

1. _____
2. _____
3. _____
4. _____
5. _____

Post Meditation Reflection: How did your meditation go?
(As well, consider writing a reflection upon owning your power as we discussed earlier.)

_____

_____

Let us meet again for Day 39 :)

Day 39

Let's start with 5 things you are grateful for in your life

1. _____
2. _____
3. _____
4. _____
5. _____

Perfect!

Now let's set an intention for today...

Intention for Day 39

Todays Mental Practice

Throughout the next 60 days there will be a meditation practice for each day. You are now on the Fourth Level of our meditation practice and today's meditation will be twenty minutes. These meditations will get longer as the days go on. Today's theme is understanding how to connect with our higher self.

"How do we connect with our higher self?"

Once you start deepening your spiritual curiosity and your wanting to be a more loving and understanding person, you will realize that it seems as if all of the events of your life had to be perfectly orchestrated to make you the person you are now and to lead you down the path you are on. You will realize your higher self or higher guidance is like an architect beautifully building a life in which you accomplish your highest possible destiny. This is because life is happening for you. You'll notice that once you become aware you'll never be able to see things the same. You'll find that the hardest part has already been initiated, and that is the awakening. I have found that even in moments in my life that involved great suffering, there were beautiful things happening at the same time that I wasn't even aware of. Only now when I look back, not as burdened by the negative emotions I was feeling, I see that my darkness was a mere lesson to teach me into being a version of myself that I needed to be. Suffering taught me compassion, negative thoughts taught me mindfulness, ignorance taught me perspective. All these lessons, but who assigns them? That's an easy answer, you. Think about it, if you could go back and choose to forego all the negative moments in your life, would you? The answer is probably no, because that's what made you who you are today. In the same way our soul or our higher self makes this choice as well before we decide to come into this life. We chose all the things we would go through because we understood that it's what we need. So in this way you need to have faith. Everything that greets you on your path, you chose. For in reality you are the path itself, and all the roadblocks as well as accomplishments you run into will be in an attempt to further show you this fact. The more we can tune into our highest frequency (love) the more we will be able to see things from a closer perspective as our higher self does. The more we destroy the limitations we put on ourselves and the more we realize how limitless we really are, the more into alignment we will come. It's always about letting go, allowing, and moving forward with love for our journey as well as the others on theirs. We must appreciate both the lows and the highs to come into balance. Love, the frequency, comes in many forms. Tapping into it may look very different than you may have suspected.

Let's practice those affirmations again! This time, write whatever feels right.

Affirmations

1. _____
2. _____
3. _____
4. _____
5. _____

Post Meditation Reflection: How did your meditation go?

(As well, consider writing a reflection upon connecting with our higher self as we discussed earlier.)

_____

_____

_____

_____

_____

_____

_____

_____

Let us meet again for Day 40 :)

Day 40

Let's start with 5 things you are grateful for in your life

1. _____

2. _____

3. _____

4. _____

5. _____

Great!

Now let's set an intention for today...

Intention for Day 40

_____

Todays Mental Practice

Throughout the next 60 days there will be a meditation practice for each day. Congratulations! You are now on the **Fifth Level** of our meditation practice. I invite you to bump up that meditation to twenty five minutes! Consider reading over today's theme: "How do you know you are meditating correctly", before entering your meditation.

"How do I know I'm meditating correctly?"

The truth is there isn't one correct way to meditate. Many things can technically be considered meditation because all meditation really consists of is awareness. Awareness of the task at hand. You can imagine if we all could always simply focus on the present task and absolutely nothing else a lot of the internal problems we deal with would cease to exist. So meditation is the act of becoming aware. When in your meditation, which I'm sure you've noticed by now, your awareness gets distracted by thoughts and you may go on a little road trip with these thoughts. Then you suddenly realize, "wait, i'm supposed to be meditating" so then you go back to following your breath. This act of becoming conscious amidst the traffic of thoughts and bringing ourselves back into focused awareness is meditation. It's the act of bringing ourselves back to center. You can carry this principle with you in your daily life as well. Your evening walk can be a meditation, simply bring yourself into the present moment. Notice as each foot touches the ground one after another, notice how the air feels as you inhale and exhale, notice what the trees or buildings look like around you. As you do this, if you find yourself again in the loop of thinking about other things, simply bring yourself back to the present. This continuous practice of bringing ourselves back into our center and tuning into the present moment is the most powerful thing we can do for ourselves. So don't beat yourself up whether you are meditating correctly, any meditation is better than no meditation. You can be lost in thought the entire twenty five minutes you are meditating and it will still be more effective than not meditating at all. For as long as you remain bringing yourself back into present awareness, this skill will continue to get stronger and you will continue to allow your brain to work for you and not against you.

Let's practice those affirmations again! This time, write whatever feels right.

Affirmations

1. _____
2. _____
3. _____
4. _____
5. _____

Post Meditation Reflection: How did your meditation go?

(As well, consider writing a reflection upon meditating correctly as we discussed earlier.)

_____

_____

_____

_____

_____

_____

Let us meet again for Day 41 :)

Day 41

Let's start with 5 things you are grateful for in your life

1. _____

2. _____

3. _____

4. _____

5. _____

Awesome !

Now let's set an intention for today...

Intention for Day 41

Todays Mental Practice

Throughout the next 60 days there will be a meditation practice for each day. Congratulations! You are now on the Fifth Level of our meditation practice. Today's meditation practice will be twenty five minutes. These meditations will get longer as the days go on. Today's theme is boundaries, and understanding why they are so important.

"Why are boundaries so important?"

We know now that we all have our own energy field, and we also know that this energy field is susceptible to negative influence as well as positive influence. This is why being mindful of what you're consuming is so important. When we talk about boundaries, the first thing to come to mind might be a friend who doesn't understand personal space, but really this idea cuts much deeper than that. As said before, our inner world is what helps create our outer world, so if we are constantly allowing ourselves to be treated badly by our own thoughts we have failed to create proper boundaries between us and the voice in our head. Change comes when we have finally had enough of being treated poorly by our own thoughts, this is when boundaries need to be set. Boundaries are again a choice of remaining conscious and aware. This line that is created between you and the voice within demands that your mind cooperate or it will be left with nothing to do. The mind hates this, the mind is meant to serve and that is all it wishes to do. When it is serving you poorly it is the result of you not taking your place in the seat of the higher self. Like an untrained dog, our minds must also be taught appropriate behavior. These boundaries that we set for ourselves within our innerspace will of course translate to outer reality. You will start to become more aware of people, places, and things that are not in alignment with the mindset you wish to uphold. In a way, certain people and things will be crossing the boundary you have set for yourself. The exact amount of respect we have for ourselves is the exact amount we will accept from other people. This is why setting boundaries is so important. It starts with boundaries you set for yourself and once that is established, you will have a more clear and concise idea of the boundaries you will hold for yourself in everyday life. Everything is always a product of how we are treating ourselves. This relationship is mirrored and projected into external reality.

 Let's practice those affirmations again! This time, write whatever feels right.

Affirmations

1. _____

2. _____

3. _____

4. _____

5. _____

Post Meditation Reflection: How did your meditation go?

(As well, consider writing a reflection upon boundaries as we discussed earlier.)

_____

_____

_____

_____

_____

Let us meet again for Day 42 :)

Day 42

Let's start with 5 things you are grateful for in your life

1. _____
2. _____
3. _____
4. _____
5. _____

Great!

Now let's set an intention for today...

Intention for Day 42

_____

Todays Mental Practice

Throughout the next 60 days there will be a meditation practice for each day. Congratulations! You are now on the Fifth Level of our meditation practice. Today's meditation practice will be twenty five minutes. These meditations will get longer as the days go on. Today's theme is consistency, and seeing how we ourselves can alter the way our mind functions.

"Why is consistency so important?"

Wherever you are in your healing journey, consistency is extremely important. If enlightenment exists I believe it's the process of healing to the greatest degree. Oftentimes it is suffering that triggers people into awakening, but it does need to be as so. You've probably suffered in your life, to the degree it doesn't matter. What matters is you deciding firstly that you want to heal the parts of you that cause you suffering and secondly you are going even beyond just healing but actually thriving. When we do things such as meditate, journal, and shadow work consistently, it creates new functions in the brain that were not there previously. Our unconscious brain is constantly learning from our actions, its only sense of self is from what it perceives. So when we truly start going the extra mile to feel better within, the brain starts to catch on. Here's the thing that throws a lot of people, just because your conscious mind knows the practice at hand and has its doubts doesn't make the practice any less effective. When you speak positively even when you feel negative, this is still adding to the algorithm your brain uses to regulate your thoughts and emotions. Our unconscious brain does most of the processing in our day to day lives, this process is not interrupted by conscious deliberation. Even if you say "I choose not to think of the color red" and then someone says imagine the color red your brain is still going to quickly show you the color red in your mind. This application works backwards as well! So even if you say "this is never going to work" while meditating it will have no disturbance on the effectiveness of your meditation. This is why you must create the space between you and your conditioning, you are not trapped and you are far from screwed. These practices work and you simply need to do them longer than just waiting for an initial response. You've spent however many years of your life thinking and acting a certain way, you think a little mediation is going to reverse all that conditioning? No, but over time it will. Just as you go to the gym everyday to strengthen your body, the same is done with your mind. You don't go to the gym once and expect to look like a bodybuilder next time you look in the mirror right? Stay consistent, it's worth it, coming from someone who has been there and has done it.

Let's practice those affirmations again! This time, write whatever feels right.

Affirmations

1. _____
2. _____
3. _____
4. _____
5. _____

Post Meditation Reflection: How did your meditation go?
(As well, consider writing a reflection upon consistency as we discussed earlier.)

_____

_____

_____

_____

Let us meet again for Day 43 :)

Day 43

Let's start with 5 things you are grateful for in your life

1. _____
2. _____
3. _____
4. _____
5. _____

Nice!

Now let's set an intention for today...

Intention for Day 43

Todays Mental Practice

Throughout the next 60 days there will be a meditation practice for each day. Congratulations! You are now on the Fifth Level of our meditation practice. Today's meditation practice will be twenty five minutes. These meditations will get longer as the days go on. Today's theme is authentic vs fake positivity...

"Authentic vs Fake Positivity?"

Firstly i'd like to say there is no such thing as fake positivity but there are such things as being inauthentic to who you are. Trying to make light of a bad situation even when you don't feel positive isn't fake. It's a conscious effort to redirect our thinking from one mode to another. Being positive isn't something some people are born with and some people aren't. It's a life skill, one that can be practiced and one that oftentimes takes a lot of hurting to know the real value of. For some people it comes more naturally, this is often people who have held onto their childlike sense of wonder, they most likely have not faced a lot of inner and/or outer conflict in their lives. This is not a negative and these people are just as special as those who I will mention now and those are people who have been through darkness and learned the value of light through their own hurting. These are the two types of people that hold on strongly to their positive mindset. Fake positivity is more of a false projection of self that one can put on. It looks more like just saying you're a positive person without having the actions to line up. For example, many people have not practiced deep introspection and like to believe they are a positive force contributing to the energy that exists in the universe. Those same people may still comment hateful things on social media, or try to shut down anyone with big aspirations, or treat people with disrespect because of opposing worldviews. Remember, unconsciousness and negativity do not go hand in hand. You are either a positive force or a negative one in this universe, whether your positivity has been born amidst you climbing your way out of darkness or you haven't experienced darkness. Of course there exists a spectrum, but the universe does not read between the lines. Never forget your essence as a being of pure energy. Energy does not lie. For one who has broken the cycles of unconsciousness this is now your responsibility as a member of society that is forging for a better future and as well as a being of energy that wishes to contribute positively to the consciousness of the planet. There are no pointing fingers, the universe is a mirror. Authentic attempts to be positive will always be better than the projection of trying to be a positive person. Intention is of utmost importance.

Let's practice those affirmations again! This time, write whatever feels right.

Affirmations

1. _____
2. _____
3. _____
4. _____
5. _____

Post Meditation Reflection: How did your meditation go?

(As well, consider writing a reflection upon authentic vs fake positivity as we discussed earlier.)

_____

_____

_____

_____

Let us meet again for Day 44 :)

Day 44

Let's start with 5 things you are grateful for in your life

1. _____
2. _____
3. _____
4. _____
5. _____

Great!

Now let's set an intention for today...

Intention for Day 44

_____

Todays Mental Practice

Throughout the next 60 days there will be a meditation practice for each day. Congratulations! You are now on the Fifth Level of our meditation practice. Today's meditation practice will be twenty five minutes. These meditations will get longer as the days go on. Today's theme is learning to zoom out and not be so emotionally involved with every situation in your life.

"How do we see the big picture?"

Energy is the purest form of currency in the universe. This is because all is energy, including us. More so, the main component that goes into creating the life we live is where we place our energy. This is why becoming conscious and aware is always the first step. A big problem with a lot of people not "getting better" is because they are still so emotionally connected to their ego. Listen, I know it's hard reminding yourself that you are a being of pure energy every second of the day, but truly this is what seeing the big picture looks like. Why do you think some people lose their cool when it comes to small inconveniences like traffic and others know how to remain calm? Well, it's really a case of seeing the big picture. You're stuck in traffic, so what? "Well I'm going to be late for my meeting?" Well you can't tell your car to fly over all the traffic so what now? You're allowed to feel annoyed but it's what you do after that really matters. Those who truly understand the way that energy and this universe operates will not allow themselves to enter a state of being they don't prefer unless it's absolutely necessary. What many people don't realize is that their emotional involvement in all the small things that take place in their lives don't allow them to live a more fulfilling life. Emotions are sacred, they are meant to be conscious of, not just thrown from one to the other. This is why something like scrolling on social media can have serious downsides, it completely disregulates your emotions. One minute you're watching a hilarious video to send to your friend and the next minute you're watching some sad video about a puppy who passed away. You have no creative energy left to give! You are not supposed to be overly emotional, this shows lack of awareness and again until awareness is met, progress can not be seriously put in motion. You need to start resonating with your higher self if you want you to live in your soul's highest alignment in this life. Key tip, the higher self understands itself to be merely an expression of the whole, of the oneness, of the universe. You need to start letting this expression align within you and it starts with self awareness as well as emotional control. If you can not control your emotions you are probably not ready for what it is you are asking for. You're a loose cannon and the universe is only a mirror! If your energy is dispersed into a bunch of different directions that means chaos is what is mirrored back to you in your life. Not chaos necessarily in a bad way, but simply what you are calling forth to you is dysfunctional. When you stop resonating with just the person you are but as an extension of all that is, magic happens. When you start to see the bigger picture, bigger coincidences and "miracles" start happening. This is what we call alignment and a big part of it is controlling your emotions.

Let's practice those affirmations again! This time, write whatever feels right.

Affirmations

1. _____

2. _____

3. _____

4. _____

5. _____

Post Meditation Reflection: How did your meditation go?

(As well, consider writing a reflection upon seeing the big picture as we discussed earlier.)

Let us meet again for Day 45 :)

Day 45

Let's start with 5 things you are grateful for in your life

1. _____
2. _____
3. _____
4. _____
5. _____

Perfect!

Now let's set an intention for today...

Intention for Day 45

_____

Todays Mental Practice

Throughout the next 60 days there will be a meditation practice for each day. Congratulations! You are now on the Fifth Level of our meditation practice. Today's meditation practice will be twenty five minutes. These meditations will get longer as the days go on. Today's theme is understanding what alignment looks and feels like.

"How do we know?"

The clearest and most concise way at navigating through our own souls guidance is listening to our body. Our body speaks in ways our mind cannot. When something is right for you it will scream yes! It will feel right, it will feel easy, it will not have to be forced. Many of us are scared to listen to this guidance due to a lack of trust in what we are doing. Many people will still have doubts. Does the universe really work this way? Am I really creating my reality? Is any of this for real? Well, how do you feel? What does your heart tell you? I can not stress this enough, the universe is a mirror. The reason I keep stressing this point is because it's easier to understand then the universe is us. Imagining the universe as a separate guidance is perfectly fine as long as you remember and keep in your heart that all is one. Everything. So your disbelief is also mirrored back to you. The power of belief is very strong. I invite you to research more into the placebo effect if you are interested in this topic because it's truly fascinating.

How do we believe?

This is a funny, yet tricky question. It is rare that something outside of you will come and prove to you that these concepts are real. This is because it is a breachment of your free will. You chose to forget, that's part of the experience here on earth. There are stories of those who have been involved in magical experiences while occupying a closed mindset which was then overtuned. They saw proof. This is something I would call divine intervention, for whatever reason and for whatever cause, this person needed to see the truth. This is not something I would bank on. Instead we can understand that belief is still a function of the mind and not the higher self/soul. The soul knows, it does not believe. So in the same way we affirm positive words to build a more positive mindset, we can also affirm the belief in these concepts. Belief itself is pure magic, as you believe so it shall be. Why? Because the universe is a mirror! It does not give you what you want, it aligns you with what you are. The truth is, more often that it isn't. That is because reality itself is a projection of the inner reality that consists of energy. So don't be discouraged if you have a hard time believing in this path, the truth is you don't have to walk it. You are free, listen to your heart and follow love not fear. Take what resonates, leave what doesn't. The truth will take on many forms to get you closer to love, because love is what is left when all else is stripped. The original energy/frequency.

Let's practice those affirmations again! This time, write whatever feels right.

Affirmations

1. _____
2. _____
3. _____
4. _____
5. _____

Post Meditation Reflection: How did your meditation go?

(As well, consider writing a reflection upon knowing as we discussed earlier.)

_____

_____

_____

Let us meet again for Day 46 :)

Day 46

Let's start with 5 things you are grateful for in your life

1. _____
2. _____
3. _____
4. _____
5. _____

Sweet!

Now let's set an intention for today...

Intention for Day 46

_____

Todays Mental Practice

Throughout the next 60 days there will be a meditation practice for each day. Congratulations! You are now on the Fifth Level of our meditation practice. Today's meditation practice will be twenty five minutes. These meditations will get longer as the days go on. Today's theme is learning the importance of leaving our comfort zone.

"Why is it important to leave our comfort zone?"

Spiritual growth within the confines of your comfort zone is similar to practicing a sport but never actually playing in a game. It can be easy to keep a positive mindset and grow in a place where we feel very comfortable. This is all good, and actually the soul grows where it is wanted and loved. Do not confuse your comfort zone for only a physical place such as your home. Though it can be just that, our comfort zone often exists within the confines of our own mind. We may be afraid to be too loud or too vocal just as an example. Someone who holds on to this fear and allows this fear to dictate where they go and what they say is still living within the confines of their comfort zone. Watch your mental process as you make decisions on where to go, what to do, and what to say. Try to be as objective as you can when monitoring your thought process and notice how fear and anxiety play their part. What don't you do that you would do if it wasn't for fear? What don't you say that you would say if it wasn't for anxiety? A good question is, if you knew everything would be alright, how would you then move forward? This question does a good job of exposing the negative belief systems we still have in place that make up the walls of our comfort zone.

How do we leave our comfort zone?

We leave the comfort zone that we have created by doing things we normally wouldn't because of fear and/or anxiety. Even if this just means saying hello and making eye contact with someone you walk by. It can be as simple as this for some and maybe more complex for others. Just because something goes against your fear doesn't make it inherently the right move. The right move will be something that excites you and that you want to do but you're hesitant because of fear. This all comes down to remaining conscious and aware. When we take the higher seat of awareness we can view our comfort zone from above, allowing us to transcend it and move past the limitations we have put on ourselves.

Let's practice those affirmations again! This time, write whatever feels right.

Affirmations

1. _____
2. _____
3. _____
4. _____
5. _____

Post Meditation Reflection: How did your meditation go?

(As well, consider writing a reflection upon comfort zones as we discussed earlier.)

_____

_____

_____

_____

Let us meet again for Day 47 :)

Day 47

Let's start with 5 things you are grateful for in your life

1. _____
2. _____
3. _____
4. _____
5. _____

Awesome!

　　Now let's set an intention for today...

Intention for Day 47

Todays Mental Practice

　　Throughout the next 60 days there will be a meditation practice for each day. Congratulations! You are now on the Fifth Level of our meditation practice. Today's meditation practice will be twenty five minutes. These meditations will get longer as the days go on. Today's theme is reflecting upon if we are truly healing or avoiding?

"Are you healing or avoiding?"

This question can be a bit complicated and one we should definitely not obsess over. This goes hand in hand with yesterday's reading that avoidance often disguises itself as growth. You can grow while turning your back to your shadow, but using this method will have its consequences. For as your light grows bigger, the shadow will as well. But this is only the case when our back is turned away from our shadow, when we face it, we immerse our shadow into our light. This may appear to darken or dim our light in the short span of things but undoubtedly the pay off is much more rewarding for we don't have to deal with a lot of our darkness at once and rather slowly chip away at it. This chipping away at our shadow truly looks like loving all parts of ourselves. For your light is love, and this light illuminates the parts of yourself that have not yet been healed or rather feel neglected. Working on loving ourselves is no easy task, especially when the conditioning for most of us does not emphasize self love as something that is necessary to thrive in this world. Not only is it necessary, it's mandatory. To say otherwise would be a key sign of avoidance rather than healing. Avoidance often looks like defensive walls that someone has put up in an effort to protect their shadow. The more defensive someone is, the more they are avoiding their own shadow. This is why many people who are in the process of loving themselves, may come off as vulnerable but vulnerability isn't a bad thing. You need to be vulnerable to accomplish anything, otherwise you're constantly defending and not creating. When you open yourself to all the dark parts of you and set the intention of being patient and loving yourself through whatever you must, vulnerability is needed. The more we avoid our shadow, the more we have to defend it. This is because it will grow and it will continue to supply demands as a result of your unwillingness to love it. It will create thoughts and emotions that force you to defend and live in a state of defense and fear. In reality all you gotta do is turn around and tell yourself sorry. Sorry for being unwilling in the past, sorry for abandoning yourself when you needed you the most. You will be surprised to find that your shadow is extremely forgiving and genuinely all it wanted was love and space to show you where it is you are hurting. Turn around, let your light cast away the shadows of your inner space.

Let's practice those affirmations again! This time, write whatever feels right.

Affirmations

1. _____
2. _____
3. _____
4. _____
5. _____

Post Meditation Reflection: How did your meditation go?

(As well, consider writing a reflection upon healing vs avoiding as we discussed earlier.)

_____

_____

_____

Let us meet again for Day 48 :)

Day 48

Let's start with 5 things you are grateful for in your life

1. _____
2. _____
3. _____
4. _____
5. _____

Great!

Now let's set an intention for today...

Intention for Day 48

_____

Todays Mental Practice

Throughout the next 60 days there will be a meditation practice for each day. Congratulations! You are now on the Fifth Level of our meditation practice. Today's meditation practice will be twenty five minutes. These meditations will get longer as the days go on. Today's theme is dealing with the opinions of others.

"The projection of others?"

Sooner or later, if you have not already, you might find yourself tasked with not letting the opinions of others bother you. Whether someone actually said something negative about you or it is social anxiety causing you to believe the people around you are against you, both create similar emotions. I understand this can be hard to deal with, especially if you feel all alone at times, but you have to remember to zoom out and see the big picture. Your emotions and the feelings you experience as a result of the judging of others will always attempt to make you feel small but you need to remember your mental practice. Everyone is projecting how they feel within themselves. Remember, if someone truly loved themselves they wouldn't make fun of another. This situation is certainly something we will have to face in our lives, and you really have to practice not caring. That's right, you have to practice not caring. Just like anything else we've discussed, some will suffer from social anxiety more than others, but the principle remains the same. It is fear and our separation from love that allows us to be casted back into the storm by the power of others. When one is operating close to the frequency of love, they see the projections of others, and they see their effort to be accepted by those who do not approve of them comes from a belief of unworthiness within them. Those who try valiantly to be accepted into a group that creates an uninviting atmosphere are also acting from a place of projection. Whether it was when we were children or whenever else in our life, a belief system that we are not worthy has been instilled deep into our unconscious. Someone who knows they are worthy of being accepted and loved will never attempt to be accepted by those who do not appreciate them for who they are. Just like any other storm the feeling may cause deep hurting, but this is an invitation for you to evolve. There are people and places out there that will value you and love you for being your authentic self. You need to love and respect yourself enough to not retaliate against those who project their pain onto you. When we surrender everything we feel in an effort to draw closer to our higher self and the frequency of love the healing process takes place quicker. Psychology and energy come into play when we examine the projection of other people's shadows, but nonetheless we are one. See beyond a person's projections and acknowledge them as also a product of love just as you. See beyond the person, see a soul lost in the illusory nature of ego and forgive them.

Let's practice those affirmations again! This time, write whatever feels right.

Affirmations

1. _____
2. _____
3. _____
4. _____
5. _____

Post Meditation Reflection: How did your meditation go?

(As well, consider writing a reflection upon the projections of others as we discussed earlier.)

_____

_____

_____

Let us meet again for Day 49 :)

Day 49

Let's start with 5 things you are grateful for in your life

1. _____
2. _____
3. _____
4. _____
5. _____

Great!

Now let's set an intention for today...

Intention for Day 49

_____

Todays Mental Practice

Throughout the next 60 days there will be a meditation practice for each day. Congratulations! You are now on the Fifth Level of our meditation practice. Today's meditation practice will be twenty five minutes. These meditations will get longer as the days go on. Today's theme is understanding how to create space for another person to heal while also helping that person.

"How can we assist the healing process?"

Some of you may be able to guess the simple answer to this question, but yes, the answer is to love them. We'll break down ways you can be of further assistance but nothing will ever be of greater help than simply loving said person. When we say loving someone, I don't mean buying them gifts, I mean channeling into yourself and creating space for that person within you. Looking at them and understanding that as an expression of love yourself, you can simply sit there and focus on loving them without any of the conditions and prejudices your mind might create. Energy always speaks louder than words. Many times in assisting someone through their storm you may feel compelled to share what you've learned. You tell them that emotions are just energy and how they are not their thoughts but most likely they don't want to hear that right now and that's perfectly ok. You will never be able to heal another person, all you could do is reflect to them their own ability to heal themselves. Likewise, you can create a loving and healing environment within yourself and this energy will invite others to do the same. Even if this means sitting in silence with a person who is hurting, you are still of service. When you serve another, you must ensure you are doing so selflessly. If your intention is to help someone who is sad, do so at a time when you do not require anything from them. Don't hold yourself prisoner to this rule for if our lives are lived completely selflessly we will end up sacrificing our own well being. It's about balance, and it always will be. There will be times you want to be there for another but maybe at a particular moment you don't have the space within you to be of assistance and that is perfectly fine. Authenticity always creates better results than aimless selflessness. You love others with the love you have forged inside of you, so it is essential you continue to forge this love within you as well as love others. Again, balance. Serve authentically.

Let's practice those affirmations again! This time, write whatever feels right.

Affirmations

1. _____
2. _____
3. _____
4. _____
5. _____

Post Meditation Reflection: How did your meditation go?

(As well, consider writing a reflection upon assisting the healing process as we discussed earlier.)

_____

_____

_____

_____

_____

_____

Let us meet again for Day 50 :)

Day 50

Let's start with 5 things you are grateful for in your life

1. _____
2. _____
3. _____
4. _____
5. _____

Sweet!

Now let's set an intention for today...

Intention for Day 50

Todays Mental Practice

Throughout the next 60 days there will be a meditation practice for each day. Congratulations! You have reached the **Sixth** and **Final level** of our meditation practice. Today, as well as the rest of the days left in our practice I invite you to meditate for thirty minutes. You got this. Today's theme is understanding that we are always exactly where we need to be.

"We are always where we need to be"

Once you realize that wherever you are is exactly where you need to be you will let go of this idea of a "waste of time." There is nowhere else to be except exactly where you are. How can your time be robbed from you when there is literally nowhere else you can possibly be. Instead try radical acceptance, for that is all one could really do. You will soon realize that even in your darkest moments, you needed to be exactly where you were to become the person you are today. There is a grand orchestration to the extent in which we can not even understand, and the only way to use this orchestration to our advantage is to learn to ride the wave of it. Instead of learning to swim and not drown in the big waves that life has to offer, we should learn to surf. Now our perspective changes. A surfer isn't afraid of big waves, actually, they chase big waves to have fun. In the same way, understand that there is literally nowhere else to be except where you are and you might as well turn this moment positive instead of dreaming of being somewhere else. Somewhere else doesn't actually exist, but where you are now does exist, and the power of the present moment is not one that is limited. Say you are sitting in traffic on your way to work. One person may lash out in anger and get annoyed remarking "I have to be at work this is bs!" While another person who is in tune with this present moment may say "ah looks like i'll be late to work." That's it. No self induced anger and stress, simply acceptance of what is. As soon as you start practicing this you will notice all the synchronicities that come about. For example, you were late to work, but when you caught that late bus to work you saw a friend you haven't seen in a while and it allowed you two to catch up. One person may say "what a coincidence" while another knows it is all in divine timing. You're always where you need to be, even if it doesn't feel obvious as to why at first. When we accept this, truly with every cell in our body, it has a transformative effect on our life. We are now riding the current of life instead of fighting it. We open ourselves to not only seeing but receiving all the miracles this universe has to offer, except they are not really miracles to those who are aware, it is simply the orchestration of life at play.

Let's practice those affirmations again! This time, write whatever feels right.

Affirmations

1. _____
2. _____
3. _____
4. _____
5. _____

Post Meditation Reflection: How did your meditation go?

(As well, consider writing a reflection upon always being where you need to be as we discussed earlier.)

_____

_____

_____

_____

_____

_____

_____

_____

Let us meet again for Day 51 :)

Day 51

Let's start with 5 things you are grateful for in your life

1. _____
2. _____
3. _____
4. _____
5. _____

Awesome!

Now let's set an intention for today...

Intention for Day 51

Todays Mental Practice

Throughout the next 60 days there will be a meditation practice for each day. Congratulations! You have reached the Sixth and Final level of our meditation practice. Today, as well as the rest of the days left in our practice I invite you to meditate for thirty minutes. You got this. Today's theme is making tough decisions and navigating our way through multiple opportunities and doors.

"Which way is the right way?"

There will be times in your life where you are tasked with making a big decision. Whether this is a major life decision or something less significant that you still value, I'd like to introduce you to a practice I use to help myself be guided by my soul. It's very simple. Before entering your daily meditation, set the intention to receive guidance from your higher self. State the two or more options you have to choose from and open yourself to being guided in the meditation and after it as well. What I have found is that not directly after or during the meditation but after a few days I start to gain a sort of clarity about what I want. I start to get extra excited about a particular choice and start to feel positive things about that choice that I hadn't previously felt. It will feel as if your choice now is a no brainer compared to the other choices in front of you.

Why does this work?

I believe this practice works on the basis of one principle. You are free to choose any path you wish at any given moment. It is a law set in stone within your life that you will have free will and free decision making. But when we set the intention to receive and when we are really in a place of being torn in two different directions and genuinely just wish to receive intuitive guidance, the soul says "let me offer you the path of least resistance." So your choice may become clear inevitably, but that doesn't make it the inherent right choice and your other options inherently bad choices, it simply means your soul is navigating you in the direction from which you can experience the most inner fulfillment. The soul will always navigate you in the direction of the most spiritual growth, that is because you in reality are soul when stripped of your outer layers. As well, the soul will continuously choose the more interesting path. Why? Because the soul is as well an extension of the universe experiencing itself, and the universe wants you to experience the most interestingly cool life you can possibly experience. This is why the universe rewards being bold, it's like watching a movie. You are going to favor movies that are really captivating and interesting. Now the universe experiencing itself through all of us, is infinitely interested in all of our storylines but when asking for guidance of how to move forward, the energy that guides you will always choose the more interesting and fun option. There is no wrong choice in the grand scheme, the universe has no agenda and will adapt to the choices you make, or that we believe we make. Like mentioned in yesterday's reading there is a grand orchestration obviously at place, so all we can do is ride that wave. Whether destiny awaits us or whether we create our own ending, all we can do is ride the wave.

Let's practice those affirmations again! This time, write whatever feels right.

Affirmations

1. _____
2. _____
3. _____
4. _____
5. _____

Post Meditation Reflection: How did your meditation go?

(As well, consider writing a reflection upon making tough choices as we discussed earlier.)

Let us meet again for Day 52 :)

Day 52

Let's start with 5 things you are grateful for in your life

1. _____
2. _____
3. _____
4. _____
5. _____

Great!

Now let's set an intention for today...

Intention for Day 52

_____

Todays Mental Practice

Throughout the next 60 days there will be a meditation practice for each day. Congratulations! You have reached the Sixth and Final level of our meditation practice. Today, as well as the rest of the days left in our practice I invite you to meditate for thirty minutes. You got this. Today's theme is vulnerability and understanding how it can lead us to greater truths and closer to the frequency of love.

"Why is vulnerability important?"

Without vulnerability there is no love, without love there is no light, without light there is only darkness. Oftentimes it is the people that have been hurt many times that will tell you to not to be vulnerable. Though they may think they are looking out for your best interest, what they are really doing is applying a handicap to your spiritual growth. When a person advises you not to be vulnerable, they are doing so from their own experiences. It is not wisdom speaking, it is pain. Life itself is vulnerable, by coming into existence all life has the chance of being hurt, but nonetheless life survives. Someone who tells you to remain closed probably isn't doing so to harm your spiritual growth, they believe they are "protecting" you from getting hurt in the future. This is how you exist in the framework of low vibrational energy. This isn't rational decision making, this is fear based decision making. This is the trade off we make, we sacrifice the chance of being hurt to experience love and grow as a soul. There is no quicker way to fall out of alignment, then to close yourself off. When you close yourself off, you literally turn your back to the flow of life. Of course it still reaches you, but you can't benefit from it because you're not open enough to receive. What you must do is this. Grow resilient within yourself and stop taking things so personal. Again, zoom out, stop getting so consumed in the base level of everything that's happening. Be rational and understand that by not being vulnerable you basically take yourself out of the game. But by centering yourself and understanding life is all about energy, you can remain open and continue to be vulnerable, this is how you become the star player. Truly kind people don't withdraw their kindness when someone is rude to them, they remain kind and don't take it personally. They understand that they can not be affected by a person's anger if they don't react back in anger. Those who are filled with love and light, those who we believe to be spiritual teachers and masters, they do not withdraw their love the second someone is mean to them. They remain loving! Throughout their lives they grow their tolerance for remaining in their light and not closing themselves off. This is where your practice lies. Not in avoiding getting hurt, but in noticing the part of you that wants to avoid getting hurt and observe and love it. Guide that part of yourself, even when it hurts and the feelings are more potent then they have ever been, breathe and remain centered. Keep yourself open, stay in the game, you are right where you need to be.

Let's practice those affirmations again! This time, write whatever feels right.

Affirmations

1. _____
2. _____
3. _____
4. _____
5. _____

Post Meditation Reflection: How did your meditation go?
(As well, consider writing a reflection upon vulnerability as we discussed earlier.)

_____

_____

_____

Let us meet again for Day 53 :)

Day 53

Let's start with 5 things you are grateful for in your life

1. _____
2. _____
3. _____
4. _____
5. _____

Perfect!

Now let's set an intention for today...

Intention for Day 53

_____

Todays Mental Practice

Throughout the next 60 days there will be a meditation practice for each day. Congratulations! You have reached the Sixth and Final level of our meditation practice. Today, as well as the rest of the days left in our practice I invite you to meditate for thirty minutes. You got this. Today's theme is allowing them"magic."

"How do we allow the magic?"

We know already that the energy we put out into the universe is that in which we will receive back. But it was never an issue of not attracting the things we wanted, it was always the problem of us getting in our own way. Naturally, once awareness is met, you should have no problem aligning with the things you want in your life. That is, considering someone who can erase all of their conditioning overnight, and that probably won't happen. Your whole life you've been told that life works a certain way, and so your subconscious holds on to these beliefs for dear life, for it does not know what would happen if these beliefs were challenged. But once you start to understand a deeper truth, and see that life is happening through us and not to us, these beliefs will be challenged. The subconscious will do whatever it can to try to bring you back into a familiar suffering rather than the unknown freedom. This is why awareness is so important, but awareness itself isn't enough. We need to learn to surrender. We need to learn from what we borrow in meditation, and that is to be nothingness. When you're so busy playing the character of you, defending your opinions, and upholding this certain character and how they're supposed to act, you leave no room for change. Not only have you bought into this illusory character you're playing known as **Ego**, you're actually pushing away the magic by defending your personhood so passionately. This is because you are attempting to control, rather than accept. You're flowing down the stream trying to swim in the opposite direction. You've got to see beyond, and you've got to learn to trust your higher self. They wouldn't guide you into anything that wouldn't assist your evolution as a soul. Why? Because they are you! But understand they are the you that is beyond fear and anxiety, and actually your higher self doesn't even understand these emotions because they operate from a frequency of love, excitement, and passion. So it is your job to get out of your own way. Learn to deal with the negative aspects of the mind and learn to see when you are self sabotaging. It is not your job to know how these amazing things are going to happen, leave the manifesting to your higher self. You just focus on being loving, present, and in alignment. Forge peace within you and act on the things that excite you because they excite you for a reason. You and your higher self come into alignment when you learn to allow. Allow the unknown, allow the universe to surprise you, and allow yourself to live without judgment of what should happen or what people should do. No more trying to control what happens next, only control how you feel right now.

Let's practice those affirmations again! This time, write whatever feels right.

Affirmations

1. _____
2. _____
3. _____
4. _____
5. _____

Post Meditation Reflection: How did your meditation go?

(As well, consider writing a reflection upon allowing as we discussed earlier.)

Let us meet again for Day 54 :)

Day 54

Let's start with 5 things you are grateful for in your life

1. _____
2. _____
3. _____
4. _____
5. _____

Sweet!

Now let's set an intention for today...

Intention for Day 54

_____

Todays Mental Practice

Throughout the next 60 days there will be a meditation practice for each day. Congratulations! You have reached the Sixth and Final level of our meditation practice. Today, as well as the rest of the days left in our practice I invite you to meditate for thirty minutes. You got this. Today's theme is understanding how to deal with negative and angry people.

"How to deal with negative individuals?"

The correct answer in relation to this topic is one that some may not want to hear but one that stands the test of confrontation. When someone comes to you in a bad mood and you can feel their energy affecting you, this is the time for you to participate in a profound practice and that is remaining in the energy you most prefer amidst the chaos of opposing energy. Understand that the minute you start to become aware of how energy underlies the reality we experience you'll start to notice how trivial it is to sacrifice your emotional well being over small inconveniences. If you were to let every negative person affect you and your state of being you would basically be living in a state of unconsciousness. This is exactly the downside of unconsciousness, it is that you are unaware of the grand scheme of things pertaining to reality so allow the everyday events of your life to affect how you feel. If someone is holding anger, there are only two ways for this energy to be released. The first option is a mindful one and an approach that we should practice when feeling the fire of anger. We simply allow ourselves space from the situation that triggered the anger within us and we allow time to run its course. We distance ourselves from decision making and allow the energy to naturally flow through us. The second and all too popular option is to release this anger with focus towards another. Whether it is towards the person that made you angry or an innocent bystander, the emotion can be released but only if it affects another individual in the process. So if someone chooses the second option on you, there is only one thing you can do to make sure their fiery energy doesn't negatively affect you. You remain in positive energy. The best thing that stops anger in its tracks is love. A close second is kindness and a valid third option is neutrality. Either way we are not retaliating back in anger and therefore not letting that energy affect us. When we do this, the person who is angry will be left with only themselves and their anger. When you retaliate on someone back in anger you are basically signing the terms and conditions allowing this energy into your innerspace. Someone's anger can not reach you if you don't allow it to. You must remain with the remembrance of zooming out and simply live with the conviction of not allowing yourself to be pulled out of your naturally light energy.

Let's practice those affirmations again! This time, write whatever feels right.

Affirmations

1. _____
2. _____
3. _____
4. _____
5. _____

Post Meditation Reflection: How did your meditation go?

(As well, consider writing a reflection upon dealing with negative people as we discussed earlier.)

_____

_____

_____

_____

Let us meet again for Day 55 :)

Day 55

Let's start with 5 things you are grateful for in your life

1. _____
2. _____
3. _____
4. _____
5. _____

Great!

Now let's set an intention for today...

Intention for Day 55

_____

Todays Mental Practice

Throughout the next 60 days there will be a meditation practice for each day. Congratulations! You have reached the Sixth and Final level of our meditation practice. Today, as well as the rest of the days left in our practice I invite you to meditate for thirty minutes. You got this. Today's theme is mindfulness and exactly how we can carry our meditation practice with us in our daily lives.

"What is mindfulness?"

I believe mindfulness is the act of treating life itself like a meditation. You will certainly reach a point in your meditation practice where you find yourself not only becoming aware of your thoughts during the thirty minutes you assign for yourself, but you also are aware of them when you are just going about the tasks of your day. This is like breaking the fourth wall and where mindfulness is introduced. Now, when we are conscious of our thinking throughout our day, we can notice negative thought patterns. Examples are judging others, comparing ourselves to others, or even anxious and fearful thought patterns that we already knew were in place. Mindfulness allows us to take the higher place of awareness at all times, or rather for as long as we can remain conscious. The ideal state of a brain is to be active and aware, yet not thinking unless you choose to do so. You're probably already aware of when you consciously choose to think something in your head versus when thoughts just come up spontaneously. It is these intrusive and unwanted thoughts that cause us our suffering. If you can choose all the thoughts you will think you would probably choose the positive and productive ones right? So mindfulness as a practice grants us the opportunity not to live at the mercy of these unwanted thoughts, instead we reside in a place of higher awareness where thoughts aren't taken at face value, and intuitive perception and processing is prioritized. The ultimate goal is to accomplish a sort of flow state for our brains to operate from. Don't confuse flow for unconsciousness though, because no thoughts does not mean flow. Flow is a state of awareness whilst still remembering where and what you are. Unconsciousness is the result of no thoughts because of distraction from life's activities. Don't stress yourself out over the curriculum too much, just practice becoming aware of your thinking. Notice the thoughts you choose to think versus those that come uninvited. This allows us to create even more space within us.

Space for people, space for miracles, space for guidance, and most of all space for love. It is only us that stands in our own way and we must simply rise above this illusory battle in the process of elevating our consciousness.

Let's practice those affirmations again! This time, write whatever feels right.

Affirmations

1. _____
2. _____
3. _____
4. _____
5. _____

Post Meditation Reflection: How did your meditation go?

(As well, consider writing a reflection upon mindfulness as we discussed earlier.)

_____

_____

_____

_____

Let us meet again for Day 56 :)

Day 56

Let's start with 5 things you are grateful for in your life

1. _____
2. _____
3. _____
4. _____
5. _____

Awesome!

Now let's set an intention for today...

Intention for Day 56

Todays Mental Practice

Throughout the next 60 days there will be a meditation practice for each day. Congratulations! You have reached the Sixth and Final level of our meditation practice. Today, as well as the rest of the days left in our practice I invite you to meditate for thirty minutes. You got this. Today's theme is allowing darkness to be darkness, and learning how the first step to transforming darkness is to stop judging it.

"How do we turn darkness into light?"

The process of alchemizing darkness into light is a powerful one. But before we can change our darkness, we must understand it. Beyond just knowing our shadow and even beyond loving our shadow comes a profound practice and that is not judging our darkness. Whether it is self inflicted inner conflict or it is the disposition of external events that led us to experiencing darkness, one thing remains the same. That is, our suffering becomes something completely different the minute we stop assigning our labels and judgments upon it. There is a misconception that "enlightened" beings don't feel darkness and don't experience conflict in their lives. It is rather a matter of the way they view this darkness in comparison to how we view it. Darkness itself isn't inherently bad, it's the opposing polarization of light. This relationship is important, for darkness holds lessons, growth, and most of all darkness allows light (you) to experience itself. Darkness turns into suffering when thinking comes into the picture. You get more out of learning to pause your thinking, then deeply thinking about something. When it comes to experiencing darkness in our lives, the feeling itself is usually bearable, but it's the constant reminders of what's wrong in our lives that's really the nail in the coffin. This is why being able to create the separation between you and your thoughts is a prerequisite to an easier flowing life experience. You can not stop the experience of conflict in your life. This is something I had to come to terms with a while ago. Whether you've experienced a lot of turmoil in your life or not, nobody wants to live within the idea that further suffering is inevitable. Well, that's because it's not true. Darkness is inevitable, suffering is not. The process of turning darkness into light is first allowing darkness to be exactly that without transforming it into suffering. This is a skill, it's called feeling and not thinking. No matter what thoughts or emotions come to you in the darker moments of your life you do not judge them and do not join in the conversation about why what you are experiencing is so bad. There is a difference between having compassion and loving yourself and pitying yourself. Never forget you are soul, you are a light, you are powerful conscious energy. Allow yourself to be empowered by this fact and see that your darkness is merely a teacher to further guide you into owning your power. Darkness is an invitation to step into our own light, it surrounds us with darkness to force us inward. Therefore learning of our power, and learning of the vast love and light that always has existed within us.

Let's practice those affirmations again! This time, write whatever feels right.

Affirmations

1. _____

2. _____

3. _____

4. _____

5. _____

Post Meditation Reflection: How did your meditation go?
(As well, consider writing a reflection upon alchemizing darkness into light as we discussed earlier.)

_____

_____

_____

_____

_____

_____

_____

Let us meet again for Day 57 :)

Day 57

Let's start with 5 things you are grateful for in your life

1. _____
2. _____
3. _____
4. _____
5. _____

Sweet!

Now let's set an intention for today...

Intention for Day 57

_____

Todays Mental Practice

Throughout the next 60 days there will be a meditation practice for each day. Congratulations! You have reached the Sixth and Final level of our meditation practice. Today, as well as the rest of the days left in our practice I invite you to meditate for thirty minutes. You got this. Today's theme is being satisfied with our own energy and how that allows us to be a magnet for the things we want in our life.

"How do we become magnetic?"

Most of us have had the experience in our lives where we enter another person's home and they have a pet. Unless the pet is overwhelmingly friendly, it usually doesn't favor someone they have never met before coming up eagerly wanting to play with them. This may upset someone who had good intentions, but they simply scared the pet away with their excitement. In this same situation, have you noticed that when either you or someone you know doesn't really pay much mind to said pet that the pet actually comes up to you. By allowing the pet space, and essentially letting them be, you actually create a welcoming and non forceful environment for the pet to enter into. The same applies for many of the things we want in life. This doesn't mean to not chase your goals, quite the opposite. Be so involved with your goals that you actually become the energy of the version of you that has already accomplished these goals. This will make you a magnet to your future accomplishments. There is an age old saying that goes by "when you want nothing, everything wants you." This is powerful and true. But this doesn't apply in its opposite form. Just because you do want something, doesn't mean it doesn't want you. The approach that is defined as having the least desires possible, is a difficult road. I believe we can take a page out of this philosophy book and apply it to our lives from a less intense degree. You become magnetic when you become satisfied with your own energy. This is often the result of practicing introspection and doing the proper inner work. When we are confident in ourselves and we realize that nothing outside of us determines our worth, we become priceless. If someone defines their worth off of appearance, money, or status, these are all things that can be stripped from you. These are labels, ones that aren't bad, but when we rely on these labels to determine our worth as a person it leaves a lesson waiting to happen per say. You are a soul, you exist beyond just the physical. Everything you need is already inside you because you are everything. Inside you lives all the love to be experienced, inside you lives all the abundance to be experienced, and inside you lives all the guidance there is to give. When you come into the magnetic energy of these beliefs and you actually begin to experience them to be the truth, alignment is realized.

Let's practice those affirmations again! This time, write whatever feels right.

Affirmations

1. _____
2. _____
3. _____
4. _____
5. _____

Post Meditation Reflection: How did your meditation go?

(As well, consider writing a reflection upon magnetism as we discussed earlier.)

_____

_____

_____

_____

Let us meet again for Day 58 :)

Day 58

Let's start with 5 things you are grateful for in your life

1. _____
2. _____
3. _____
4. _____
5. _____

Great!

Now let's set an intention for today...

Intention for Day 58

_____

Todays Mental Practice

Throughout the next 60 days there will be a meditation practice for each day. Congratulations! You have reached the Sixth and Final level of our meditation practice. Today, as well as the rest of the days left in our practice I invite you to meditate for thirty minutes. You got this. Today's theme is understanding the power of silence.

"Why is silence so powerful?"

Silence in many ways holds a lot of answers. In fact, many of our internal problems stem from the fact that we simply can't sit in silence with ourselves. Hopefully you have been following the daily meditation practices and are starting to see a difference in this regard. Words, in the form of speaking and in the form of thinking are oftentimes not the best mechanism used to describe how someone feels or what someone experienced. It is this need to explain and rationalize everything that keeps us within the bounds of limited spiritual experience. When you start meditating more often and start thinking less, you learn to involve yourself with a deeper type of intelligence, intuition. This is why the process of learning paired with the clearing of the analytical mind leads to a rewarding outcome. Silence has a way of communicating that is beyond language. Whether you have noticed yet or not, you are being guided by this silence. It sits and waits for you patiently, and when you become one with the silence you feel peace. Us being able to turn off our thinking mind temporarily can be seen with the analogy of a wave finally breaking on the shore and returning to become one with the ocean. When we briefly come into our place of awareness and create space between us and the character we play, we come into harmony with the natural peace and flow of nature. You can imagine another analogy that your mind when you are overthinking is like the ocean in high tide. You keep getting dragged to shore with every wave, you have no time to remember you are not the waves, you are the ocean. When the mind becomes silent, you can imagine an ocean with very low tide. No waves at all, just a peaceful ocean existing in stillness. This is what the process of tapping into silence is like, when you create the ability to silence your thoughts, you tap into the intuitive intelligence and guidance of the whole ocean. For this frame of understanding, the ocean is consciousness. Thoughts are created from consciousness, but consciousness is not created from thinking. Consciousness is the ocean, and thoughts are the waves.

Let's practice those affirmations again! This time, write whatever feels right.

Affirmations

1. _____
2. _____
3. _____
4. _____
5. _____

Post Meditation Reflection: How did your meditation go?

(As well, consider writing a reflection upon magnetism as we discussed earlier.)

_____

_____

_____

_____

Let us meet again for Day 59 :)

Day 59

Let's start with 5 things you are grateful for in your life

1. _____

2. _____

3. _____

4. _____

5. _____

Perfect!

Now let's set an intention for today...

Intention for Day 59

_____

Todays Mental Practice

Throughout the next 60 days there will be a meditation practice for each day. Congratulations! You have reached the Sixth and Final level of our meditation practice. Today, as well as the rest of the days left in our practice I invite you to meditate for thirty minutes. You got this. Today's theme is understanding how love is applied to people and the present moment.

"Love for Others, Love for the Moment"

Love is appreciation, not attachment. Love is unconditional, not dependence. For the final reading of our journey, I'd like to leave you with something you can carry with you past just this book. We've already talked about the one question you can ask yourself to see how far you have strayed from being in alignment with your soul, that is, "how far have I strayed from unconditional love?" This isn't something easy to do by any means, but if you would like to see how close you are or how far you are from being in alignment, that is the only question you have to ask. Love for others looks like love without the conditions of normal human relationships. Real love, the frequency of creation, is not dependent on anything to exist. That is because love is the core energy/frequency of reality. When you think of life's natural direction, such as a river flowing downstream, you can imagine the same for the natural flow of life from which we cannot see. There is a flowing stream of energetic consciousness that flows in the direction back to its source, or where it came from. So, we can again use the analogy of water. A river may go on for many miles, but eventually it will once again reconnect with the ocean. This is similar to the journey we go through in our lives. Many of us go most of our lives swimming upstream. We defend the ideas and beliefs we have been told for dear life, not realizing this is holding us back from experiencing fulfillment. The point of all messages and all messengers, was to love first, then learn what you must on that path. When we give up looking for the rational truth of reality, and rather just surrender to love, we begin to finally flow with the stream. It's as if after making this acceptance to love, the universe says "finally, now the fun can begin." Life itself is a product of the universe's love for itself. We, the sum part of the universe, love ourselves enough to come here and separate ourselves from our natural state. There is only one ocean, there is only one consciousness, and it is love. It is oneness, it is joy, it is peace. We exist in the frequency of love itself, and we descend here to experience the varying emotions of existence. Whether you have experienced a taste of this frequency yet or not, choose the path of love and growth and you will be sure to. Remain with an open mind and open heart. Greet each coming moment as a welcomed guest. For this moment is new and unknown, but you my friend have been here all along. Your energy, your love, your light, you have been here since the beginning and you will continue to experience your own process for which you have designed for yourself. We are not experiencing the present moment, the present moment is experiencing us. Love this moment, and the one that follows, and watch as your relationship with reality changes. You and the life you live start to dance, you start to love this life and this life is so grateful for your love. When we do not fear or judge the present moment, and instead love it no matter how it looks, the universe as it unfolds becomes comfortable expressing itself to us. For it knows that we are aware, and it knows that we will love it and serve it unconditionally.

Let's practice those affirmations again! This time, write whatever feels right.

Affirmations

1. _____
2. _____
3. _____
4. _____
5. _____

Post Meditation Reflection: How did your meditation go?

(As well, consider writing a reflection upon magnetism as we discussed earlier.)

Let us meet again for Day 60 :)

Day 60

You have done it my friend, you have completed your sixty day journey and I am proud of you. I hope you have learned, grown, and loved throughout these sixty days. I now ask you to write a reflection of your whole journey.

What's one key point you have learned through this experience?

_____

_____

_____

_____

_____

Are you ready to love yourself? Are you ready to let go of old thought patterns and habits that no longer serve you? Are you ready to continue your healing journey? Are you ready to become who you were destined to be?

_____

_____

_____

_____

_____

_____

_____

Now I leave you, but this is not goodbye. You can find me on all social media platforms @kinzer.mb. This is not the end, in fact, it is only the beginning. So now I leave you with the same question I greeted you with sixty days ago...

Are you ready to begin?

Made in the USA
Middletown, DE
13 September 2024

60916805R00137